Bette Davis

...Her Film & Stage Career

Bette Davis

...Her Film & Stage Career

Her hair is Harlow gold
Her lips sweet surprise
Her hands are never cold
She's got Bette Davis eyes.
D. Weiss and J. De Shannon © Warner Brothers Music
Used with permission

JEFFREY ROBINSON

PROTEUS
REELS

LONDON · NEW YORK

PROTEUS BOOKS is an imprint of
The Proteus Publishing Group

United States
PROTEUS PUBLISHING CO. INC
733 Third Avenue
New York, NY 10017

distributed by
THE SCRIBNER BOOK COMPANIES INC
597 Fifth Avenue
New York, NY 10017

United Kingdom
PROTEUS PUBLISHING LIMITED
Bremar House
Sale Place
London W2 1PT

ISBN 0 86276 022 4 Paperback
ISBN 0 86276 032 1 Hardback

First published in 1982

Picture Credits
All photos except for the following, courtesy of the Kobal Collection: page
15, 25, 26, 46, 81, 89 courtesy of the National Film Archive Stills Library; page
108 Rex Features and page 112 Columbia Pictures Television

Editor Kay Rowley
Art Direction B-blunt & Associates
Design Baillie Walsh
Filmset by SX Composing Ltd, Rayleigh, Essex
Printed by Printer Industria Grafica sa, Barcelona, Spain
D.L.B. 30587 – 1982.

Contents

The First Chapter

THIS IS NOT A BIOGRAPHY.

The story of Bette Davis' life is hers to tell. The men she married, the men she loved and the lives of her children . . . all of the happiness and the loneliness . . . that story belongs to her. She's told part of it in *The Lonely Life* and another part of it in the sequel she titled *PS*. She's told the world everything she wants it to know and the rest just isn't anyone else's business.

But Bette Davis is a woman who has earned a very special place in the history of American cinema and that story belongs to all of us. The story of those films, of an artistic career that spans half a century, all of it comes together in this filmography. A guide to Bette Davis, the first fifty years. A sort of filmgoers' companion to more than seven-dozen movies . . . some good, some bad, some worth forgetting, some so memorable that they can't be forgotten . . . a kind of road map marked with sights well worth stopping to see. At the end of 1981, exactly fifty years after she first went to Hollywood, the American show business trade paper *Variety* printed their list of "Hit Movies On U.S. TV Since 1961". With thousands of films to choose from, they had gone back over two decades of ratings to come up with the most watched films on American television. They compiled twenty years worth of prime time viewing and no less than four of the films starred Bette Davis. *Hush . . . Hush, Sweet Charlotte* was her most popular. *What Ever Happened To Baby Jane?* came next followed by *The Catered Affair* and *The Nanny*. If you're still in doubt simply check the *New York Times* clipping file on her. It's enormous and cross-referenced into several boxes stuffed with cuttings. There is more on her in the *New York Times* "morgue" than there is on some American Presidents. At the British Film Institute Library in London there are literally dozens of entries under her name. In dusty shops, buried away on narrow streets, where they sell cinema memorabilia . . . posters, stills, autographed pictures, books, postcards and that sort of thing . . . when you ask for anything about Bette Davis, you get a shrug. Sold out, they tell you. Or, if there is anything, the price will be high. The collectors of such things don't let her memorabilia sit around to gather dust.

A two-time Academy Award winning "Best Actress", she's been nominated no less than ten times. Film students put her work under microscopes. Late night film buffs go to work bleary-eyed the morning after one of her epics from the '30s or '40s runs its last reel at 4 a.m. Small art theatres do record business when they show a classic Bette Davis double-feature.

But none of this should come as any surprise. After all, when someone once asked movie mogul Jack Warner to define the term "movie star" his two word answer was "Bette Davis".

That's Bette, as in Betty. Only the British call her Bet and the people who do usually find themselves on the receiving end of a lesson in pronunciation. She won't let you get away with calling her Bet in much the same way that she's never let anyone get away with anything that's concerned her career. She got to the top because she was willing to fight her way there. And fifty years later she hasn't given up the fight. Sure there are a lot of talented actresses running around but the difference between Bette and the rest of them is simple . . . she's a survivor.

"I am foolhardy enough to tackle anything that I regard as a challenge," she wrote back in the mid-'40s. "I have not started a picture without wondering whether I could do it. I did want to try, however. This is not because of any fantastic belief in my ability but, rather, because I am in a highly competitive profession in which it is worse to fail through timidity

A publicity shot from the Thirties.

than audacity. The theatre and the screen are only for those who love struggle. Hollywood is the goal for millions of girls and boys. Possibly there are several courses to the affluence, prominence and satisfaction that the screen affords. The one in which I believe is the one I followed. Hard work."

It really wasn't until the mid-'40s that serious film critics began to figure her out. Until then it seems she was something of a mystery. They didn't quite know what to make of her. She won awards in the '30s but she wasn't a very pretty girl in the Hollywood sense of the word glamour. Her blonde hair wasn't blonde enough. She didn't like to show her legs. Her eyes might have been Bette Davis eyes but no one penned songs about such things way back then. As British film critic Peter Noble wrote about her in those days, "She became a star mainly on her acting ability, for she is not, by the usual standards, a great beauty. She has a good face and the most expressive eyes and mouth in Hollywood; so intense are some of her portrayals that she almost wills you to believe that she is superbly beautiful. And indeed there are moments in many of her films when she looks almost breathtakingly lovely."

He credits that loveliness to, "A powerful inner fire, a sort of emanating radiance which one feels was possessed by those great ones of the drama."

At various times, some of her early critics accused Bette of playing with "Too much brain and too little heart." But Noble wasn't one of them and he didn't hold back when he said what he felt time alone would prove. "When the full history of the first twenty years of American talking pictures comes to be written the name of Miss Bette Davis will possibly loom the largest. Bette Davis is, without doubt, the finest feminine representative of the American school of screen acting."

In the Summer 1947 issue of *Stage and Screen Magazine* Noble wrote about her talent at great length. He began by describing the 1931 version of Bette . . . the twenty-three-year-old girl from New England who went to California with stars in her eyes, a girl with "mousey hair and an unassuming presence" whose film debut was "a small part and inevitably, she passed unnoticed." Sixteen years later her talents were finely tuned and her reputation as a great actress absolutely secure. "She possesses an astonishing capacity to excite admiration in her audiences and to compel full attention for the part she is playing. Often her roles are melodramatic, sometimes they are obviously written to suit her magnetic personality but as an ardent admirer I can say, and with it echo the thoughts of many filmgoers, that she is one of the most supremely satisfying film actresses in the American cinema."

Peter Noble was also the man to call her, "The first lady of the American screen," a title which has followed her ever since. It was certainly the sentiment echoed by the Associated Press in 1954 when they wrote her obituary.

As is the custom with well known people, press services and newspapers sketch the lives of the famous so that should the need suddenly arise, a complete story can be put together in time for the next morning's paper. Bette was only forty six at the time and in good health but the Associated Press was taking no chances.

Hers was Sketch No. 3907, dated November 1, 1954. It began, "The brilliant career of actress Bette Davis gained added lustre from the perseverance and hard work on which it was founded. To reach the top she had to overcome a series of setbacks and disappointments. These beset her before she even got started."

Of course the obituary left room for the obvious last minute news but then it went on to trace her early years as an aspiring actress. By the time Bette reached stardom AP pointed out, "Many rated her as the screen's best dramatic actress. She was one of the highest paid performers. The Treasury's list of the nation's leading money earners for the calendar year 1946 gave Miss Davis top billing for her sex. Warner Brothers paid her $328,000 before taxes. Her earnings during twenty-two years in Hollywood were estimated in 1953 at around $3 million.

AP explained how in 1949 Bette announced her "professional divorce" from the Warner Brothers Studio so that she could find, "A wider choice of stories than is now possible at any one studio." They said she could easily have stayed with Warners, secure in the fact that she was big box-office but that she believed in taking chances.

"You've got to take chances," she always preached, "if you want to achieve anything in the arts. You can't play it safe."

The fact that she did take risks is one of the things AP says made her unique. "She gambled in many turns of her career. After playing ingenues, she took a chance on the unattractive waitress role in W. Somerset Maugham's *Of Human Bondage* and that had an important part in shaping her famous career. Miss Davis chanced a secondary role in *The Man Who Came To Dinner* because she felt she needed a comedy. When many top names in the movies shunned television, she did a comedy TV show with Jimmy Durante and even helped put on the commercials."

On top of that AP claimed that Bette was never concerned about the size of her roles. "It would be a good thing," she was quoted as saying, "if we got rid of the star system of Hollywood that requires an actor's role must be big and fat. No wonder the English pictures are so much better acted than ours. It's because the finest performers there are not afraid to take smaller roles, so long as they are good ones."

They followed that remark by returning to the idea that Bette had to fight her way up the ladder and that the way she accomplished it was by never turning down a challenge. "It was hard to leave behind the people you had worked with so many years," she said. "They seemed like a family. In fact, I saw a lot more of them than I did my family. But it was a challenge. It's good to break the ties and seek new experiences. The next six months were a difficult period though. I had a 'lost' feeling and wondered if anybody would ever want to hire me."

Among the films AP felt worthy of mention were *Bordertown, The Petrified Forest, Dark Victory, Juarez, The Old Maid, The Private Lives Of Elizabeth and Essex, All This and Heaven Too, The Bride Came C.O.D., Now, Voyager, Payment On Demand, Beyond The Forest* and *The Star*. They described *All About Eve* strangely enough as "A satire on Hollywood" which it certainly doesn't seem to be today and made sure to mention that the New York Film Critics gave it their 1950 "Best Movie" award. They also awarded Bette their "Best Actress" award for that year. AP then noted, "Popular polls conducted by French trade and movie-goer magazines picked Miss Davis as the best foreign actress for her role in the same film."

She is erroneously credited with seventy-five films through 1954 when the actual figure should be sixty-five. She didn't make her sixty-sixth film, *The Virgin Queen*, until 1955. There was, however, mention of her 1952 return to Broadway. After twenty-two years in Hollywood Bette opened in the musical review "Two's Company", labelled by AP as "One of her few attempts at comedy. In it she did comic roles including a hillbilly sketch, shimmies and a cooch dance at a reported salary of $3000 a week." But the play was dogged by bad luck. "When it opened in Detroit, prior to the Broadway première, the star fainted from the strain of rehearsals though she came back five minutes later and resumed her role. The opening in New York was delayed by cast changes and extensive revisions of material. Then Miss Davis became ill and the opening was further postponed. A few weeks after the show opened she was taken ill again. 'Two's Company' closed after eighty-nine performances. . . ."

While the show was still running AP must have asked Bette if there were any differences between stage work and film work because they quoted her as saying, "There is no difference in the mediums. If you're an actor, you're an actor. It doesn't matter whether it's stage, pictures, television or radio, you're still acting. This matter of 'going back' to the stage is ridiculous. You don't 'go back' to the stage. It's merely a matter of geography. Acting is acting in any medium. The English are lucky. They can do plays and pictures without travelling. They don't talk about 'going back' to anything. It would be the same in this country if the movie industry were on Long Island instead of Hollywood."

The obituary ended on a personal note. "In 1932 Miss Davis married band leader Harmon Oscar Nelson Jr. They were divorced in 1938. Two years later she married Arthur Farnsworth, a businessman, who died in 1943. Her third marriage in 1945 was to William Grant Sherry, an artist. They had a daughter, Barbara. That marriage ended in divorce in 1950 and that same year she married Gary Merrill, her leading man in *All*

About Eve. Besides her daughter, Miss Davis has two adopted children, Michael and Margo. During World War II, Miss Davis was active in the Hollywood Canteen which she helped to organize for the entertaining of service men."

Five years later journalist Thomas Wiseman wrote a piece about Bette where he painted a picture of her as a fighter, as a woman who had always known what she wanted and had always been willing to do battle to get it. He felt that Bette had never been one of those "girl next door" types, that she was of a different vintage. "Fine old Brandy rather than lemon squash. If nothing else she has a rarity value. There is nobody else like her, nobody else with those swamp-like eyes which grip you and don't let you go." He gave her a lot of credit for being, "A woman who has never aspired to be beautiful," saying she compelled attention. "By the sheer brute force of her acting. She twisted our arm and we went quietly. In her twenty-five years as a star she has wept enough tears to float an aircraft carrier, she has suffered every trauma in the textbook and inflicted a few herself. In the grip of some emotion, love, hate, desire, revenge, she has churned up the screen like a harpooned whale. She is the Goddess of unrequited love."

They met when she was fifty years old. By that time she had made sixty-eight films, the most recent having been *The Catered Affair*. Her days of playing the ingenue were far away, having long since, settled into playing those very tough roles, the ones that these days might be called "Bette Davis characters." She had undeniably mastered her craft yet she told Wiseman, "Nobody ever told me that I was divine. The Warner Brothers didn't believe in that technique. At MGM they believed in the red carpet treatment for their stars. At Warner Brothers you were just workmen. I suppose in the long run that was the better way of the two though I should have liked to know what it feels like to be told that one is divine."

Wiseman then quoted Bette as claiming that she was never interested in doing anything that was easy and right there he hit upon a major point. "To be pretty and get somewhere on that would never have suited me inside. Besides, I didn't really have much choice about that. I was the first star who ever came out of the water looking wet. I had to fight for that. Katherine Hepburn had the same fight. I never cared a lot about how I looked. In silent films you had to look like film stars. I was fighting to be allowed to look like people. When I was thirty I played Elizabeth the First who was supposed to be sixty. I played her as she was then, bald and without eyebrows. Of course I didn't mind. I never gave a thought to how I looked."

It was, Wiseman felt, shock therapy for her fans. During the early years of Hollywood audiences were used to seeing film stars in glamorous roles. Then along came Bette and audiences eventually responded overwhelmingly to her brand of realism. "To see Miss Davis aging for her art, something she did with almost masochistic relish, was a sight not to be missed. She never spared the wrinkles."

Bette answered him with, "It's a sad plight for a woman who has been beautiful and sought after to find her whole world crumbling away as she grows old. But it is not a problem that I have had."

When Wiseman asked if there was anything Bette might have regretted about her life or her career, he got this slightly surprising confession. "I would have liked to have done more singing and dancing and developed my career along that line a little more than I have." She added that at one point during the '50s, she had given serious thought to the idea of retiring. "I made great plans to give it all up. But then I changed my mind. I decided I would keep my hand in for the discipline. I've seen those women who've given up everything, sitting around, driving everyone mad because they have so much energy and nothing to do with it. So I decided I would continue. But it isn't a great driving force with me any longer, not the way it was. There isn't anything I want to prove now."

In the early '60s Bette once again proved she was a fighter. She felt her career had taken on a dull lustre. She knew the difference between great scripts and mediocre scripts and that she was not being *offered* any great ones. So she set the film industry on its ear by doing something no actress of her status had ever dared do before. In

September 1962 she took out a full page ad. in *Variety* and *The Hollywood Reporter*. It read:

SITUATION WANTED
Mother of three (10, 11 and 15). Divorcee. American.
Thirty years experience as an actress in motion pictures.
Mobile still and more affable than rumor would have it.
Wants steady employment in Hollywood.
(Has had Broadway.) Bette Davis. References upon request.

Some people in Hollywood felt Bette had gone too far. They thought it was undignified, that the ad. was in bad taste, and that even in Tinsel Town you never admitted you needed work. Yet when it came to her career she has never been one to be talked out of something once she'd set her mind on it. The ad. did what she wanted it to do. Hollywood remembered she was alive. Hal Humphreys at the *Los Angeles Times* went to see her before the noise quieted down and she told him, "That ad. simply threw down the gauntlet to this town and it accomplished its purpose. But you still can't be box office without a good movie. The star is always blamed when a picture flops and I had too many bad pictures."

She had eventually, grown weary of constantly being invited to play old ladies. The straw that really broke the camel's back was the offer she received immediately following her success in *What Ever Happened To Baby Jane?* Burt Lancaster was doing a film called *The Unforgiven* and he rang Bette to ask her if she'd play his mother. She must have hit the ceiling. "I just don't feel like Burt Lancaster's mother," she said to one interviewer. Nor did she feel like the fifty grandmother roles she had been offered around the same time. She was, however, more than happy to appear on TV as a spinster in *The Virginian*, to sing and dance on the Andy Williams Show and to pinch hit as a lawyer for Raymond Burr one week when he couldn't make his usual appearance on Perry Mason. But no, she wasn't going to play Burt Lancaster's mum. Anyway, she told the *LA Times* that Baby Jane had "resuscitated" her career. "The telephone rings again and even Warner Brothers wants me back." But she knew the business and was shrewd enough to understand that in spite of Baby Jane and the Situations Wanted ad. the chips were always riding on the next spin. "If my next picture isn't good then I'll be back where I was." And pictures were where the future lay. Television, she said, only called upon the old stars when things got tough. "They prefer these young kids who don't know anything. The rest of us know too much and are demanding for that reason. But when TV productions are in a bind they call on us because we know our job."

Hal Humphreys asked if she had ever thought about retiring and her answer is somewhat different from a few years before. "Frankly, if I didn't have to work, I would be just as happy keeping a home." But Humphreys wouldn't buy that and he ended his story about her by saying, "Bette picturing herself as the happy hausfrau is the only statement she made which doesn't make sense. It's highly unlikely that she ever will be found making domestic science a career or that we'll have to ask what ever happened to Bette Davis?"

Probably the most interesting line in that particular interview is ". . . if I didn't have to work . . ." After all, this was once the highest paid woman in the United States. And while Hal Humphreys let that remark slip by, AP reported James Bacon didn't. When he interviewed her the following year he asked her point blank if a star of her magnitude actually did have to work. With characteristic frankness she told him yes, that she had never invested her money in things like real estate the way so many other people in Hollywood tended to do. "I never thought that artists should be business-men. The minute an artist looks at a cost sheet, some of the spark is lost. I could have bought half the San Fernando Valley for $30 an acre but I didn't, my work would have suffered."

That, she said, was one reason for the Situations Wanted ad. "For eighteen years at

Warners all the scripts were written for women. Then writers started writing for men and we were out. A few producers like Ross Hunter made pictures for women *and* made money with them but the town was still a man's world." She hinted that it stayed that way for her until Robert Aldrich came along with Baby Jane and insisted that the leads be played by Bette and Joan Crawford. "And he fought for us, even when producers said 'Who in hell wants to see those two old bags in a movie?' "

In that same interview she spoke just as candidly about her private life. "An actress is a machine, a driving, a powerful, one-way machine. No one can run her career for her. Invariably she will choose the man who is least apt to interfere with that career. Unfortunately such a marriage is destined to end in divorce and regrets. We can't help it, that's the way we are. It's such a shame to feel this way because I really like men. I'm a New England puritan so I shall never cruise from lover to lover."

Bacon then moved on to the subject of age. He wanted to know what she felt about getting older. "I accept age cheerfully," she told him, although years later in an interview with British journalist, James Cameron-Wilson, she would contradict that statement. "I am one of the few women of my era whose career was not based on glamour or sex. People came to see me act which should prove something, that the audiences are not children, else I would never have made it." Bacon suggested that anyone who ever saw Bette with Humphrey Bogart and Leslie Howard in *The Petrified Forest* might easily mistake her for a sex symbol. But she said no. "Cameramen spoiled us. They made us all look more attractive than we were."

That was 1964 and for the first time in nearly a quarter of a century Bette made four films. First came *Dead Ringer* with Paul Henreid as the director (in England the film was called *Dead Image*) then *The Empty Canvas* a film she did in Italy for Carlo Ponti. *Where Love Has Gone* came next followed by *Hush . . . Hush, Sweet Charlotte*. Somewhere in the middle of it all she found the time to talk with Louella Parsons.

"You don't carry on a conversation with Bette Davis," Parsons wrote, "you ask a question and then duck. It isn't that Bette doesn't want to hear your viewpoint, it's just that she has so much to say on any topic you toss into the conversational ring that it may take a while to get around to your turn." The doyenne of Hollywood columnists felt that the film Baby Jane had sparked "a box office riot" and rekindled Bette's career but Bette said she was still fighting for important films and scripts of quality. "It's a slow process and has to be taken step by step. Fifty per cent of this town felt Baby Jane was a freak. Everything I've accepted since hasn't been the greatest but there was always a reason."

Bette went on to tell Louella Parsons that doing *Dead Ringer* was an especially gratifying experience because it was done at Warners where she hadn't been very welcome for a long time and where at various times she was snidely referred to as "the fourth Warner Brother". Shooting *The Empty Canvas* in Europe, however, turned out to be a much less pleasant than she had hoped. "An absolutely traumatic experience. Pictures abroad I found impossible because of the language barrier. Also, there is no discipline in the way I know discipline. It just isn't as peppy as our work." She returned to the States for *Where Love Has Gone* although it was not quite the role she was looking for. Then she found Robert Aldrich at her doorstep again. He wanted her for what otherwise could have been the sequel to Baby Jane. But, as Parsons pointed out, Bette was not of the same mind. "She was determined that *Hush . . . Hush, Sweet Charlotte* should not be a sequel to Baby Jane and she won out. Everything about it is different. The story, characters and the location. It's no coincidence that Bette Davis' pet quotation is 'I have fought for what I believed in all my life so why not one more fight!' "

Louella Parsons was certainly right about not always getting in a word edgewise with Bette as Richard L. Coe found out when he interviewed her for his "On The Aisle" column in the *Washington Post* of November 9, 1965. "Has no one any taste any more?" She started off all by herself. "I've seen those awful new plays in London and New York and some of those code-less movies." This was about the time when nudity and harsh language were breaking through the barriers. "They're awful.

They're boring. Actors shouldn't put up with them." "The way for any actor with taste is to let things get rolling for a week or so on a movie and then just refuse to say such lines or to do stupid, tasteless things. By then the producers are so in hock they'd have no choice but to follow the actors' tastes."

She told Coe she found taste in England equally dubious. "As for those London plays some critics have praised so highly, we don't have to put up with that junk over here. It's about time the United States got proud, damned proud of what we have. We've always taken a back seat to Europe, and it's time we stopped. The Europeans know better themselves. They admire the good American movies. Always have. It's the synthetic junk that's so appalling. Name me a really true sex symbol in today's movies. Of course not. She doesn't exist. Fakes, all of them."

Coe probably just sat there taking notes because Bette went right on. "Taste, that's what's lacking and where do you find it? Marilyn Monroe was a real sex symbol and so was the great Garbo. They didn't need to say things, they just were. They photographed. That's so much of it. Take Gertrude Lawrence. There was glamour incarnate on the stage. She didn't register a thing on the screen and she took that hard."

When Coe finally got around to it he described Bette as "A miniature of her screen self and for all her forthright opinions is utterly, shatteringly feminine." But by that time she was on to another subject. "*The Nanny* is the last of my trio of horrors and I think for what it is, and horrors aren't easy to do, it's good. I've always been sorry we had that head rolling out of the box in *Sweet Charlotte* but life is filled with mistakes, isn't it? I suppose I made a mistake when a very polite emissary came to ask me if I would play a small role in the re-make, the second re-make, of *Of Human Bondage*. I said no, so politely, so quietly that I surprised myself. What I should have said was yes, if I can write just one line. The line would have been when I opened a door, looked at her and said, 'My Mildred, how you've changed.' "

Rex Reed didn't get away much easier when he spoke to her for her sixtieth birthday. "Don't send flowers, I'll be in bed all day," she told him. Then she started on another theme. Reed let her go. "Let's face it," she said, "no one's writing scripts for older women. Everything is youth oriented now. When I was fifteen or twenty years younger, I got all of Miss Bankhead's or Miss Barrymore's parts from the stage but if you want to stay with your profession you have to stay up with the times. This is the age of horror films. The world is pretty horrible. So I did four or five pieces of crap in a row." Suddenly she changed gears. "I used to hate my face when I was young but now I'm glad. It's a blessing. But I never kidded myself into thinking the crap I made was really art in disguise."

She explained to Reed that some of those films, the ones she called crap, she's never bothered to see. Yet every now and then one shows up on television. "To remind me I didn't fight hard enough. But all that is over now. I'm not rich but I don't need money as much now as I used to so I no longer need to make crap."

Then she asked Reed if he knew what had ruined the film business. Without giving him much of a chance to respond she said, "Actors. They'll walk across the screen for anything but I'm the only one of those dames who kept her price. My price for putting my name on the marquee is $200,000 and ten per cent of the gross and I won't even talk to anybody for anything less because when they see me on the screen they're seeing thirty-seven years of sweat. They pay for my experience and if that loses its importance, *I* might as well get lost."

Times have changed, she went on, but not necessarily for the better. "Today all the fun is gone in making movies. In the old days we had time to be individuals. You don't even get to know the men on the crews any more. How do you think I got all those great camera angles? I was right there behind the camera lining up the shots."

But that's not the only thing she thought was different. She said in the old days scripts were written for stars. She and Humphrey Bogart, for instance, worked together in her first film when they were both unknowns but they couldn't work together once they were both major attractions. "In those days one star had to carry it alone and they were not eager to waste us on each other's properties. So I never worked with Cooper, Gable, Grant, any of the real kings of the screen. They had their films and I had mine."

In 1962, Bette published *The Lonely Life* and true to form she told it like it was. Twelve years later, Whitney Stine, a self-confessed long time Bette Davis fan, wrote *Mother Goddam*. He sent her the manuscript and asked her to pen in her own comments wherever she wanted to. He then incorporated them into the text and they make the book come alive. They give the biography a neat helping of spice which so many previous books about her lack. One of the points that runs through Stine's book is that Bette has always had a reputation for being tough to deal with when it came to her career. Right after the book came out Tom Donnelly of the *Washington Post* asked her about that. Immediately she fired back, "I was no monster on the set and I can show you quotes from a lot of actors I've worked with that prove it. I wanted to see things done right, yes. I wanted costumes and make-up to fit the character, yes. I wanted scripts to make sense, yes. I suppose there was a great deal of jealousy about my career, because let's face it, it's been quite a career and I suppose it makes a better story to have me carrying on like Catherine the Great or somesuch."

When he asked her whether or not there was any truth to the stories about her early days in Hollywood, the stories that had people forever saying that she had about as much sex appeal as Slim Summerville, her answer was, "I'd never been considered a dog back East. Drat it, I was an attractive girl. I had plenty of beaux. I had ash blonde hair but that was considered brown in a land that was swarming with brightly bleached imitations of Jean Harlow. I could never have been a Harlow but Perc Westmore, a make-up genius at Warners, knew what he was doing when he advised me to lighten up a few shades. It had the effect of making me look like myself for the first time in films."

Donnelly also asked her about the changes she's seen in screen work between the early days and now. "Today," she said, "don't let anybody be caught acting, for heaven's sake. They don't write big scenes any more. They don't write scenes, period. I was the luckiest woman in the world. For maybe ten years they brought me wonderful scripts. They were really stories. They gave me things to do, emotions to express, situations to get my teeth into. Hollywood didn't used to be afraid to show larger-than-life people."

Bette herself has always been one of those larger-than-life stars and in 1977, when the American Film Institute gave their Life Achievement Award for the very first time to a woman, that woman was Bette. A few days before the gala at the Beverly Hilton Hotel Gary Arnold, the *Washington Post*'s film critic spoke with her. She told him that if she were just starting out in the movie business today she might give the whole thing a second thought. She said that these days the opportunities were too limited and the support too shaky, especially for women. "It just happened and no one has devised a system to compensate for the changes. Perhaps we shouldn't complain. We had wonderful opportunities for more than twenty years. Maybe it's just the actors' turn to dominate for a generation. The themes and problems seem so much more formidable and violent now. They overshadow the content of most of our pictures which usually had a romantic conflict at their core and were designed to appeal to a large, faithful audience of women. Those films don't seem adequate now but I'm not sure what can replace them. They certainly can't have the impact of the conflicts one sees in the mens' vehicles."

He broached the subject of the Warners' contract system and she told him, "I resisted certain assignments violently but the contract system was the greatest system in the world for the movie public. We were constantly making films and the public got to know us. It's distressing to see how little regard for their profession or identity many young performers have today."

Some of those young performers play multiple roles in the making of their films, working not only as actor but also as director or producer or editor or writer or score composer or any combination of the jobs that go into a movie production. Bette tried producing once but that was a flop for a number of reasons so she settled for just being

'One of the only two stars to come out of Hollywood who knew how to smoke' – the other was Bogart.

15

an actress. It was more than enough for her. "There's only so much any one person can do," she claimed. "It's difficult enough fulfilling your responsibilities as an actor or actress. I can't understand how anyone can function as producer or director or whatever at the same time. It sounds impractical. In the first place, I've never felt that actors were the best judge of their own acting. If you're working with an intelligent director you can trust him to select the best takes. It only becomes a problem when you've got a weak or incompetent director."

The night of the gala was March 1, 1977. Taped for television, the evening was broadcast on CBS three weeks later with the opening line "Fasten your seat belts, it's going to be a bumpy night."

Jane Fonda played host and when her father got up to speak he pointed out that it took "two Fondas to honour one Davis". Throughout the evening film clips showed moments from her greatest roles. Throughout the evening the people who knew her best told the world why they loved her. William Wyler, for instance, who directed her in such memorable performances as *Jezebel* and *The Little Foxes* said that Bette was difficult to work with, "But not in the usually accepted sense. She was difficult in the same way I was difficult. She wanted the best and to get it nothing was too much trouble. Sometimes she wanted more takes on a scene than even *I* did." But then he added, "No one I know brought more heart and devotion, more energy, honesty, integrity, ability, professionalism, more sheer damn hard work to a marvelous career than she did." The others called her wonderful and kind and generous and a legend. She accepted it all with a great deal of humility taking the podium to say that the Life Achievement Award was really the frosting on the cake of her career. And, she said, she had four people to whom she owed so much thanks. The first was actor George Arliss who gave her a role in *The Man Who Played God* and in some ways saved her career. Next came Jack Warner. "I think he finally did respect me. He said so once, anyway." Then she thanked Hal Wallis who produced no less than eighteen of her films. "Unbelievable opportunities he gave me as an actress." And finally there was Wyler because she thought of him as the director who made her "A box office star." The evening ended with Bette falling back on a line from *Cabin In The Cotton*. She looked out over the room filled with friends and told them all, "Ah'd love to kiss ya but I just washed ma hayah."

The evening was pure Bette Davis and after it aired, *People Magazine* described her as "Anything but the camp grotesque the impersonators make of her. She's tiny with rather skinny legs and of course, those incredible, heavy-lidded blue pinball eyes."

In that article, written by Leroy Aarons, she admitted to a side of herself that only a few people have ever seen. "I'm aggressive but curiously passive. I had to be in charge and I didn't want to be. I was more vulnerable than anyone would care to believe." Aarons finished his story by quoting a remark by Hal Wallis. "She was tough but she never played 'star'. Fortunately she had the talent to go with her demands."

In many ways the picture of Bette was rounded out still further a few years later by British journalist James Cameron-Wilson who interviewed her while she was filming *Watcher In The Woods* for Disney. She was, he wrote, "A woman with a sense of humour and a will of iron trying patiently for the umpteenth time to disprove the rumour of her own bitchiness." She told him, "I never said I fought the system. I said I fought the scripts." And with that she explained, "I've never been a waspish or acid-tongued person but I suppose professionally I have been a very outspoken woman."

She was seventy-one years old at the time and probably because of that they spoke about age. This is where she contradicted something she once said about growing old gracefully. "On my thirtieth and fortieth birthdays I found it murder to cope. On my fiftieth I just said, 'Well, here we are.' On my sixtieth, I found it positively frightening. And on my seventieth, I officially went into mourning." That was all very much in line with what she told the *New York Times* the previous year. "Nuts to growing old. Don't ever believe that life begins at forty or that it's wonderful to be seventy. I'd give everything to be thirty again. Every so often somebody asks me if I've had my face

Her first film – Bad Sister.

lifted. I always tell them, 'Would I look like this if I did?' "

More recently, Bertil Unger interviewed Bette on the eve of her fiftieth anniversary in movies, describing her like this: "Her large eyes seem to pop a bit, she speaks in capital letters, stressing every word, underlines the syllables, punctuating with exclamation points and various marks that are not found in grammar books." And they too spoke about age, as Bette confessed, "A great deal of the applause I get these days is because of my age. I guess audiences may be surprised I can still walk across a stage at seventy-three. I think it's stupid to lie about your age. If you have any kind of facility left at seventy-three, I think you can be very encouraging to young people."

Then Unger asked if she had any regrets. Now she said, "My one regret is that I am by myself at this time. It would be very nice to be living with a husband I had known for twenty or thirty years."

And if that's her only regret, note that it's about her personal life, not about her career. The point is significant because when you look at her career, when you look at it really closely, there doesn't seem to be much reason why she should regret anything. There might have been a few parts she'd have gladly played or a few people she would have been happy to work with, there might even have been a few pictures she would just as soon not bothered to make but regrets . . . no . . . and she sums that up quite well in *The Lonely Life*. "If you aim high the pygmies will jump on your back and tug at your skirt. The people who call you a driving female will come along for the ride. If they weigh you down, you will fight them off. It is then that you are called a bitch. I do not regret one professional enemy I have made. An actor who doesn't care to make an enemy should get out of the business. I worked for my career and I'll protect it as I would my children, every inch of the way. I do not regret the dust I've kicked up. I always fought people my own size, and more often than not, they were bigger."

Bette -

Getting There

SHE WAS BORN RUTH Elizabeth Davis on April 5, 1908 in Lowell, Massachusetts. The family house was on Chester Street. As the story goes either her sister couldn't pronounce Ruth Elizabeth or, to avoid confusion with her mother whose name was Ruthie, she became Betty. The spelling of her name didn't get changed until somewhere around her first year in High School when a friend of her mother's, who had been reading Balzac's *La Cousine Bette*, suggested Betty drop the "y" and add the "e" because that would set her apart. Years later when Bette read the novel she realized what a horrible creature Balzac's Lisbeth Fischer was. All the less flattering when you consider that Balzac was obviously making a pun of the name, which in French is pronounced exactly like the word *bête* which means beast or sometimes even fool.

Because there are already enough biographies chronicling Bette's youth, the world doesn't need another one. Enough has already been written about her childhood, her relationship with her father, her mother's divorce, her stay at boarding school and the period she, her sister Barbara and her mother spent vagabonding around New England.

One of the stories from her childhood, however, stands out because it had a marked effect on her later career. It was probably the first time she ever wore a costume. She was about ten. There was a Christmas party at the Crestalban School in Berkshire Hills, Mass. and Bette was playing Santa Claus. The tree was decorated with candles and at one point she must have moved too close for her costume caught fire. Her face was burned badly enough for Ruthie to spend the next several weeks wrapping and unwrapping bandages, bathing her blistered skin with boric acid. Years later Ruthie would remember, "That's when Bette's eyes got big. It had something to do with the boric acid. The irises became enlarged. The eyes the world knows." That accident also permanently affected Bette's facial skin, making it forever sensitive to wind, sun and some kinds of theatrical make-up.

In the summer of 1925, after moving from New England to New York and New Jersey and then back to New England, Bette began to study dance with a woman who called herself Roshanara. Originally from England, her real name was Jane Cradduck, and she was considered by some to be a brilliant dancer. She was also the designer on George Arliss' production of *The Green Goddess*. Bette's first performance for Roshanara at the Mariarden School of Dance in Peterboro, New Hampshire was as a fairy in *Midsummer Night's Dream*. Director for that performance was a man named Frank Conroy. Next she appeared as a moth in a dance number where she wore a silk gown with enormous wings. And that's when she got her first taste of applause. Today she says, "I remember the excitement of performing that night in front of an audience. The applause thrilled me."

It was during that summer that Conroy, a professional actor, went to Ruthie Davis and made an often quoted statement. In Bette's autobiography she says that Conroy told Ruthie, "You must see to it that your daughter goes on the stage. She belongs there. She has something which comes across the footlights." In other books about Bette, Conroy is quoted as saying things like, "If you don't put that child on the stage, it will be a crime. She has something you can't buy. Something that makes your eyes follow her even when she doesn't speak. And when she does, it is just added excitement." Whatever the actual remark was, the important thing is that Bette turned some of her attentions toward the stage and Ruthie seemed to have done everything possible to encourage her.

There might have been several plays in high school, Bette says in her autobiography that she can't remember the name of her senior year play, but at least one of them was Booth

Bette Davis at 17.

Tarkington's *Seventeen* in which she played Lola Pratt, opposite Harmon (Ham) Nelson, whom she would eventually marry. At about the same time, on a visit to Boston, Bette saw Blanche Yurka at the Jewitt Playhouse in Ibsen's *The Wild Duck*. It was the first time Bette had ever been to what is sometimes referred to as "the legitimate theatre" and she left thinking that the part of Hedvig was one she'd love to do. Little did she know at the time just how that part would advance her career.

After graduation from High School, Bette decided the next step would be acting school. In *The Lonely Life* she reports going to New York in September 1928 to meet Eva La Gallienne whose repertory company was then "one of the bright hopes of the theatre". The date, however, seems to be a mistake. Based on the dates of work she did with stage companies over the next few years, it should probably read September 1927. In any case, Eva La Gallienne turned Bette down after their meeting because she thought Bette not serious enough about acting. The school that proved Eva La Gallienne very wrong was the Robert Milton – John Murray Anderson School of the Theatre. A few weeks after the La Gallienne rejection, at Ruthie's insistence, Bette was interviewed and accepted by Anderson. He was a sometime playwright/producer who later remembered Bette as, "A quiet, modest, ambitious, unattractive yet definitely talented youngster whose diction was perfect."

When the semester opened, Anderson himself gave the class of seventy students a lecture about the actor's life, how tough it was and how it was constantly filled with hardships. He all but forgot to mention anything about the glamour. Bette described that lecture as, "The most discouraging pep-talk ever delivered to a group of novices." By the end of the term, however, the scores of little society girls had folded up their tents and only twelve students remained. That's when one of the instructors, George Curry, told the group, "If anyone really wants to be an actor nothing can discourage him. A real artist brings his own conviction and hope. He may be encouraged along this line. He cannot be discouraged. If you stuck this term out you've at least got the stuff."

A lot of people had passed through the school as students, including Joan Blondell, whose name then was Rosebud Blondell, Lucille Ball, Paul Muni and Ceasar Romero. Visiting lecturers were the stars of the day, including George Arliss who advised the students to avoid the fashionable 'British theatre' diction. And the dance teacher was a woman named Martha Graham. A long time later, when talking about the way certain actresses walk, Martha Graham would be quoted as saying that among dramatic actors, it was Bette Davis who always best expressed emotion by using her full body, the way a dancer does. Bette answered, "If this be so, I would like to remind her that it was she who made it possible. Every time I climbed a flight of stairs in films, and I spent half my life on them, it was Graham step by step."

Towards the end of term, Bette won the role of Sylvia Fare in the school's production of *The Famous Mrs. Fare*. It was directed by James Light of the Provincetown Playhouse on MacDougal Street in Greenwich Village. She had, however, developed a cold that week and on the evening of the performance she had a mild case of laryngitis. The play called for the actress to change from a sweet girl at the beginning of the play to a bitter and corrupt woman by the close. By the third act Bette's voice was terribly hoarse and she could just about get through the final speeches. It appeared that Sylvia's decay was complete. The entire audience naturally assumed that she had put on the whisky-baritone voice and a good many people in the audience told her that they were stupified by her vocal range. She didn't add, but thought, 'So was I".

Impressed with her work, Light offered her her first professional engagement but it meant that she would have to leave school. On his promise she quit but unfortunately, the play never even went into rehearsal and not only was she out of work but now she was also out of school. She got in touch with Frank Conroy and he suggested she speak with a young producer/director in town to cast a play for the Lyceum Theatre in Rochester, New York. Conroy even wrote a letter of introduction. The producer/director was George Cukor and his Cukor-Kondolf Company had one role left in its production of a play called *Broadway*. It was the smallest part of the play and, either because he couldn't find anyone else or because he believed in Conroy's recommendation, he hired Bette.

As a chorus girl she had one line but, by the time she went on stage opening night, she claimed to have learned to say that single line in nearly two dozen different ways.

What happened next is a story she's often told. On her mother's psychic advice, Bette secretly understudied the role of Pearl. Ruthie, it seems, had a premonition that the girl playing Pearl would break her ankle, which is what happened. Cukor looked around for a replacement and there was Bette. He asked if she could learn the part by the next morning. Seeing that she already knew it, she quickly assured him that she could. The following night she played her first leading role. But she was nervous about it and the result is one of those neat stories that only comes out of the theatre. Her leading man was Robert Strange and early in one of the acts Bette was supposed to shoot him. She was to pull the trigger twice and he would stumble into the wings through a convenient door, meaning that he wouldn't have to lie on stage "dead" in front of the audience for the rest of the act. But Bette has always had a phobia about guns and that, coupled with her first night jitters, went right to her trigger finger. She kept firing. Being a good actor Strange reacted accordingly. He couldn't stagger away, filled with that much lead, so he dropped where he stood and lay on stage for what must have seemed to him like an eternity until the curtain came down.

At the end of the play's run, which lasted until the end of the week, Cukor engaged Bette as the ingenue lead for the company's next season. She then returned to New York and started pounding the pavement looking for a casting director who would give her work. Eventually she was given the name and address of a man who said he was the producer of The Cape Playhouse in Dennis, Mass. on Cape Cod. She didn't think it strange when she went to the address and found the man, in his hotel room, greeting her in an undershirt and with a beard full of shaving lather. The meeting didn't last very long and he said she was hired. He gave her a date to be at the Playhouse and the name of Raymond Moore, the director.

The Cape Playhouse was, like many summer stock companies around America, a repertory group where a visiting star came in weekly to fill major roles around the permanent cast. Bette knew this would be a wonderful opportunity but when she finally arrived ready for work, Raymond Moore doused all her hopes by saying that the man in New York had no authority to hire anyone and anyway, all the places were full. Begging for work, she explained that she and her mother had already rented a house nearby, that they had no money, and she had no idea of what else she could do. Out of sympathy, Moore hired her as an usher. It turned out to be a lucky break for both of them.

That summer she did one play with a group *The Junior Players*. It was called *The Charm School*, presented in East Dennis as a benefit for a local church. But it was an amateur production and for a while that looked like it would be the only acting she would do all summer. Then came A. A. Milne's *Mr. Pim Passes By*, directed by and starring Laura Hope Crews. The part of Dinah called for an English ingenue and Crews claimed that no one in the regular troupe was capable of playing it. She insisted that someone be sent up from New York. Moore was the one who suggested she speak with Bette about the part. She offered it to Bette but only on the condition that she learn to play and sing the English ballad "I Pass By Your Window". This was supposedly Saturday afternoon. Bette and Ruthie drove all over the Cape looking for the sheet music. On a hunch, Ruthie finally found a church organist who in fact knew the song. Bette studied it non-stop that weekend and sang it for Crews at the appointed hour on Monday. Thirty years later she claimed she could still remember every word of it.

During rehearsals Crews, however, grew slightly annoyed at the way Bette waved her arms whenever she spoke. To stop her Crews gave Bette a sharp slap on the wrists. It was an acting lesson that helped turn Bette's performance into a success. She was given a resounding ovation. As the audience of the Playhouse was on a subscription.

They seemed especially delighted with their usher turned into an actress. Moore was also delighted and invited her to return the following summer as the company ingenue.

Although the dates are not clear and exact records of those performances do not seem to exist, it may also have been the summer when Bette stepped into the leading role in the Playhouse production of *The Silver Chord*. She had understudied the part and, after one rehearsal, carried it off to the point where the director, a man named Harold Winston, said she was "quite a promising young actress".

When the summer ended Bette returned to Rochester in up-state New York, where the Cukor company had moved into new digs at the Temple Theatre. George Cukor, of course, would eventually go on to legendary heights in Hollywood, directing such films as *The Philadelphia Story, A Star Is Born* and *Gaslight*. But now he was only in his early thirties and, in a sense, still learning about direction. The first play that year was *Excess Baggage* starring Wallace Ford and Miriam Hopkins. It was followed with *Cradle Snatchers* starring Elizabeth Patterson and Marie Nordstrom; a play called *Laff That Off, The Man Who Came Back* with Harlan Tucker and Charlotte Winters; *Yellow* with Louis Calhern and *The Squall*.

"I won't say our season was distinguished for drama," she eventually wrote, "but I was learning my trade. There's no doubt about it, working in a stock company will always be the greatest foundation for an acting career. An actor tackles a new part each week and there's no time for nonsense. The necessary discipline can be found in no other place, plus the confidence and the technique that is gained. Crises are met and conquered. A tempo is created and sustained. The constant tension either makes you or breaks you. Every actor knows stock can make you slick rather than profound but you can't play a concerto until you know your scales. There's nothing wrong with facility, no matter what the arty-crafty claim. Stock gives an actor facility. It makes him a professional. He can go on from there. Nothing can teach you to act like acting."

She took her work very seriously. Perhaps even too seriously because right after *Yellow*, and just before *The Squall*, Cukor fired her. Without explanation he told her she was through. She now supposes that the reason was because she didn't socialise with the company but at the time she didn't know. Calhern, in an interview many years later, explained "She was so grimly dedicated to work that it became boring. Of course, that dedication took her further than any of us but it didn't make for comfort in an incestuous company like that. She was a terrific team player but wasn't a team person. I think Cukor yielded to pressure in getting rid of her. She was very unpopular."

The reviews in Rochester, whilst only mentioning her very briefly, had nevertheless been flattering. The word "promising" kept being used so she knew she was on the right track. And while thumbing through the trade papers, she read that James Light was casting for *The Earth Between* at the Provincetown Playhouse. Ruthie suggested Bette get in touch and when she did Light wrote her that yes, he could use her.

Written by Virgil Geddes, *The Earth Between* was the story of Nebraska farm life and the relationship between a farmer and his sixteen-year-old daughter. Bette was cast as the daughter and says she was so naïve about life in those days that she never saw the incestuous overtones in the play. Light himself didn't explain anything about them to her and, in a sense her innocence helped her portray the part correctly. An old hand at the theatre . . . the Provincetown was where Eugene O'Neill got his start, as did Paul Robeson playing in *The Emperor Jones* and *All God's Chillun Got Wings* . . . Light knew how to get his plays reviewed. His formula was simply to hold the opening night on an evening when no other theatre had one. He did this with *The Earth Between* and managed to lure the critics downtown. The next morning, Brooks Atkinson in the *New York Times* gave Bette good marks for being an actress with "A soft, unassertive style". The critic for the *New York World* disliked the evening but stopped short of panning the play completely by saying that it was well acted, "especially by Miss Bette Davis". The *New York Daily News* spoke about, "Miss

Davis, a wraith of a child with true emotional insight". The play ran for its scheduled four weeks and was, by all standards, considered a hit.

During those four weeks a man came to see Bette on behalf of Blanche Yurka who was appearing uptown in *The Wild Duck*. It seems that Yurka was taking the show on tour but the girl who was playing Hedvig would not be going. Bette naturally jumped at the chance. A meeting was arranged and at the end of it Yurka gave her the role. Suddenly finding herself playing the role which launched her love for the theatre, Bette went from Manhatten to Queens then on to Philadelphia, Washington D.C., Boston, Newark, New Jersey and back to Manhatten where the show closed at the Shubert Theatre on 96th Street and Broadway.

In addition to playing Hedvig on that tour, she also had the role of Boletta in the company's alternate production of *The Lady From The Sea*. Her work in those two plays won her praise wherever she played. *The Philadelphian* wrote "The strikingly effective portrayal in the production is that by Bette Davis in the role of the daughter ... Miss Davis thrills us". *The Washington Post* said, "Especially commendable was the selection of Bette Davis, a talented ingenue with a native sweetness and spiritual wholesomeness that blends ideally into a lovable character. Bette Davis is a young woman who is going to advance far in her stage endeavours." And the *Boston Traveler* added, "Miss Davis manages to wring this emotional part dry of its dramatic content, without lessening Miss Yurka's role, and what a feat that is."

Returning to the Cape Playhouse for the summer of 1929, she had parts in plays such as *The Constant Wife* which starred Crystal Hern, *The Patsy* which was her first comedy and George Bernard Shaw's *You Never Can Tell* starring Dodd Meehan. When that season ended she went back to New York, acquired a theatrical agent named Jane Broder and found a pair of offers on her plate. The first was for a role in the touring company of *Saturday's Children*, the second for a role in a new play by Martin Flavin called *Broken Dishes*. It was to star Donald Meek and Bette got the ingenue lead. A dramatic comedy, even then considered fairly unpretentious, Meek was the henpecked husband, Eda Heineman his overpowering wife, and Bette the daughter. The play previewed on Long Island, moved to Brooklyn and finally opened on November 5, 1929 at the Ritz Theatre on Broadway. The reviews were favourable. Bette's salary was $75 a week but that was doubled after three months and the run of the play eventually went to nearly two hundred performances.

One night during that run, Arthur Hornblow Jr. sat in the audience at the insistence of Samuel Goldwyn who had wired him from Hollywood to find out about Bette. He had seen her reviews and thought she might be perfect for a film he was producing for Ronald Coleman called *Raffles*. He wanted her for the role which eventually went to Myrna Loy. Another version of the story was that he wanted Bette for a film called *The Devil To Pay*. Whichever, after seeing her on stage, Hornblow invited her for a screen test at Paramount Studios in Astoria. It was a disaster. The lighting was wrong. The direction was wrong. Her make-up was wrong. The costume was wrong. She was uncomfortable in front of a camera. And when Goldwyn saw it he reportedly shouted, "Who wasted my time with this one".

Years later, Bette looked back on it by saying, "it has always been a wonder to me that Hollywood ever discovered anyone from a screen test. Evidently they proceeded on the theory that if the result was even remotely favourable, there was no end to the glories that could emerge if the studio accepted you and really went to work on you." And about that first screen test she said, "By mutual unspoken consent, the test was ignored by everyone. It was brutally clear that the movies were not for me."

When *Broken Dishes* closed in the Spring in 1930, she went back to the Cape Playhouse for her third season, believing that in the fall she would rejoin Meek and the rest of the cast on a road tour with the play. During that summer she played a variety of roles at The Cape, unfortunately just which ones have been lost to time. Most of her biographers get the progression of her stage work wrong anyway, juxtaposing the dates of her work with Cukor and the plays of the first two seasons at The Cape Playhouse. The chronology used here is by far the most logical, based on reviews, and mentions in her autobiography of related dates.

In the fall, the *Broken Dishes* company played Baltimore and Washington D.C. After just one week Bette received a frantic call from producer Oscar Serlin who needed an actress immediately for the female lead in his new show, *Solid South*. It starred Richard Bennett and originally his daughter Joan was to play opposite him. But she had commitments in California and now the role was open. Whilst Bette didn't necessarily want to leave *Broken Dishes*, this meant another chance on Broadway.

Bennett was Major Follensby. Bette was his granddaughter Alabama. It was the first time she had a chance to try out her southern drawl, an accent she would use many times again.

Solid South however did not turn out to be much of a success. The story line was not particularly strong but it might have survived longer had it not been for Bennett's bad temper. On the second night, for instance, after having received bad reviews for the opening night he spent part of his curtain call lashing out at the critics. Then, as the week wore on, he turned his anger towards the audience when they didn't respond the way he felt they should or when they laughed in the wrong places. At times he even stepped out of character in the middle of a scene and made aggressive comments to the audience. Needless to say, Bennett didn't win the play a lot of friends. Bette's reviews were all right but she wasn't a big enough name or a big enough attraction to keep the play afloat. It closed after two weeks. Yet it was during those two weeks that she was contacted by Universal Studio's talent scout, David Werner. He had a screen test to offer her and this time she knew better than to jump at it. She insisted on better lighting, better make-up, better costuming and better direction than she had had the first time. And this time she got it right. Carl Laemmle, Senior, who owned Universal, saw the results and offered her $300 a week plus round trip expenses to come to California. The contract would run three months with options to renew every three months for a year.

She signed in David Werner's office in New York but before the ink was dry he supposedly said to her, "I just don't know why I have done this. You are the greatest gamble I have ever sent to California. It's quite obvious that you are not the kind of person who is usually a success in pictures. You don't look like any actress I have ever seen on the screen."

Bette must have been quite shocked to hear this. But then Werner confided to her, "Yet for some reason I cannot analyse, I think I am right. I am sure that you will go a long way in Hollywood."

Little did he know.

She might have thought that was the end of the lecture. It wasn't, because Werner was also the person to give Bette her first advice about life in Hollywood. "You're going to find Hollywood a strange place," he said in what, these days, would be called a gross understatement. "One thing you must change is your manner of dressing. Don't be so conservative. Dress gaily and colourfully so people will notice you. I hate to say it, but you will realise I am right. If you are to be accepted as a movie star, you must dress and act like a movie star, at first anyway." It probably wasn't until Bette got to see Ruth Chatterton walk on to a set that she came to understand first hand what Werner meant.

So she left New York, destined not to return to the stage there for over twenty years. Strangely enough, when she did return, although she'd dress and act like a movie star, she would never again have a success. But then when she and her mother left for the West Coast on December 8, 1930, very few people believed she'd have much of a success in films. Five days later when she stepped off the train in Los Angeles, filled with hope for the future, she looked around for the press photographers who always greeted actresses in Hollywood and no one seemed to be there.

Top left – as a baby. Top right – with her sister Barbara (left). Bottom left – as a moth for a dance number, Summer 1925. Bottom right – In the Provincetown Playhouse production of The Earth Between *with Grover Burgess, March 1929.*

Bette Davis · Grover Burgess

The Beginning Years

UNIVERSAL STUDIOS IN 1930/1931 looked very much like a Hollywood movie lot was supposed to look. White washed buildings that had a vague Spanish style to them served as offices. Large, sloping-roofed hangars were the sound stages. Streets where buildings only had fronts were used for outside shots in one film then signs like Acme Bank were repainted to read Hoover General Store and the same street was used again for another film. The public was kept off the lot by a huge gate that bore the studios name across it. Laemmle Senior, referred to as "Uncle Carl" was a European born gentleman, a dandy of sorts, complete with a fresh flower in his lapel every morning. It is not quite clear from everything written about those days, however, if he, like the other film magnates of the era, was more interested in making movies or making money. One thing is sure, he was extremely interested in keeping his family employed. Even distant members of the clan were given jobs at Universal and at one point as many as six dozen Laemmle relations were said to be on the payroll. The most obvious one was Carl Junior whose main job was being the boss' son. As is often the case, it was the father who created the empire and he was the dynamic one. It was the son who inherited the money and that's all. Carl Junior was the studio boss whenever his daddy would let him play at it and it was his idea to put Bette in the Universal production of Preston Sturges' play *Strictly Dishonorable.* At least that's what he planned to do until he saw her face to face for the first time. Then, he didn't know what to do. Somewhere in the rule book, he was sure, it was written that Hollywood actresses were supposed to be glamorous. The best he could say was, "The trouble with you is that you're homely. You'll never get ahead. You have about as much sex-appeal as Slim Summerville." The remark was, of course, unfounded and Bette was, not unreasonably, insulted by it. The problem was that Laemmle believed it. He couldn't imagine giving her a break. But she had a contract and she was going to cost the Laemmles $300 a week for the next three months. From Bette's viewpoint, $300 a week was not all that much money to live on in Los Angeles . . . some people were known to be making upwards of $5000 a week in those days . . . and three months was not all that much time to prove herself to the world. But from Carl Junior's viewpoint he was stuck with her. As she herself described it, "From the time I arrived they treated me like a poor cousin. I soon learned that in Hollywood you are treated according to your salary scale. Added to this, I soon found that I did not exactly inspire the Universal executives to give gasps of delight on seeing me."

Hardly. Laemmle decided she would never do in *Strictly Dishonorable,* so he gave her part to Sydney Fox. It was an especially shattering blow to Bette's ego. Then the Universal executives went into a huddle. They had to come up with a way to save their investment. One solution would have simply been to write it off, to pay her and send her home. She had a name on Broadway and she could easily go back to that. But someone who saw her Universal screen test came up with the bright idea that the test didn't show her legs. Maybe, they reasoned, if they tested her again and she had great legs they could more easily find parts for her in upcoming projects. So they put her in front of the cameras and told her to lift up her dress. She demanded to know what legs had to do with acting ability, and the test director told her, "You don't know Hollywood."

She did what she was ordered to, but she resented it. When she saw the test she fled from the projection room, ran home to her mother and announced that she wanted to leave Hollywood. Had she made that announcement in front of Carl Junior, he might well have let her go and her career would have ended right there. But Ruthie managed to talk Bette out

Bette Davis c. 1930.

of being too rash and she decided to stick it out because going back to New York as a "loser" was not to her taste. The studio publicity department in the meantime had come up with the brilliant idea of changing her name. They wanted to give her something sexier than Bette Davis and suggested Bettina Dawes. They argued it had a lot more flare than her real name. She thought it sounded too much like "Between the drawers" and absolutely refused. That battle she won. The next one she lost. Laemmle sent her to be tested again, this time for a possible part in a Walter Huston film called *A House Divided*. It was to be directed by one of the Laemmle relatives, William Wyler. She was sent to the costume department but they didn't have anything that properly fitted her and when she arrived on the set, her dress was much too low cut. Laemmle Junior had already made his opinion of Bette well known on the lot and had remarked to some people, "I can't imagine anyone giving her a tumble." Wyler, when he saw her dressed like that, remarked for all to hear "What do you think of these dames who show their chests and think they can get jobs?" She and Wyler would meet again and then things would be different. But in 1931 she was merely a 5ft 2in ashen blonde in a world of much taller, much blonder girls. She wasn't yet Bette Davis, superstar. She was simply a plain girl from the East Coast whose talents were as yet unknown.

Carl Junior finally came up with a part for her in a film called *Bad Sister*. Based on Booth Tarkington's story *The Flirt*, it was a remake in sound of a Universal silent film from 1924. That, by the way, was typical of what was going on in Hollywood during those first few years of sound. Studios used sound to remake their silent hits and while many of those silent hits today seem to be wonderful efforts of another era, a lot of those sound remakes are often best forgotten. *Bad Sister* is a good example. Sydney Fox played Marianne, a spoiled little girl so bored with the attentions of her suitors that she falls for Valentine, a small town con-man played by Humphrey Bogart. Bette is Laura, Marianne's less than exciting sister, who is secretly in love with Dr. Lindley who is played by Conrad Nagel. Lindley, however, is very much in love with Marianne. Valentine eventually dumps Marianne who eventually dumps Lindley. He then finds true happiness with the ever-faithful Laura.

Playing the good sister didn't turn out to be very easy for Bette because the odds were stacked against her. She found the dialogue wooden, Hobart Henley an especially uninspiring director and she didn't care much for Humphrey Bogart. She said Bogart's usual behaviour was ill-mannered, he often showed his bad temper, drank too much, and was generally speaking, a bore. Nor did she care too much for Sydney Fox as the film's star. "I was so virtuous, so plain, so noble and so saccharin," she wrote about those days, "that it turned my stomach. All that nobility and what did it get me? The second lead." The only thing she had to console herself with was, "At least I was going to work." But then, when it came to making her work easier, it didn't seem that anyone cared. "According to all existing Hollywood standards, my face was not photogenic. Embarrassment always made me have a one-sided smile and since I was constantly embarrassed in front of a camera, I constantly smiled in a lop-sided manner. My hair, my clothes, my God. They hadn't cared. It was as if they dared you to be good. No one bothered to help me." Not that work conditions in those days exactly inspired great acting. For the most part they did nothing to alleviate a novice's fears. Cameras were stationary and microphones were enormous. Actors had to play to the camera and the microphones. Sound stages were supposed to be completely sound-proof, but this was before air conditioning. The lack of air together with the heat from the lights made conditions impossible. In this particular film, the sound engineers decided the best way to mike Bette was to sew one of those enormous microphones into her clothes. That made movement very difficult and because the mikes were as inefficient as they were large, every time she turned her head the wrong way, the dialogue was lost. The *New York Times* seemed to feel that the film disappeared "In the general shuffle of adapters, dialogue writers and modernizers".

She was used to doing her own make-up for the theatre and, since no one seemed to be willing to do it for her in Holywood, she did it here too. But stage make-up and film make-up are not the same and the result of her efforts in this film prompted one critic to remark that she looked like, "Something that had been left out on the front porch for the Salvation Army".

Then there was the problem of working with Conrad Nagel. She had seen him many times before in films and by this point in his career he was something of a national heart-throb. He made her nervous. One scene in particular was especially nerve-wracking. She had to play it with Nagel while giving a baby a bath. The idea was that she would bathe the child, diaper it and then kiss Nagel. "The scene oozed goodness," she said, "as Conrad was to watch my wholesome sweetness." To the list of virtuous, plain, noble and saccharin, now add naïve. She was bothered by the scene not merely because of Nagel but also because of the baby. She didn't know if it would be a boy or a girl. And everyone around her sensed her discomfort. The afternoon they were to shoot, all of her co-stars showed up to watch. The baby was brought in wrapped in a blanket, then unwrapped and handed to her naked. Of course, it was a boy. "I thank heaven that Technicolor was still to be perfected," she said years later. "I played the whole scene in a deep blush."

She and her mother went to the film's opening night and the two of them had reason to blush. It was pretty awful. Laemmle Senior saw the film and his feeling was "Can you picture some poor guy going through hell and high water in a picture and ending up with her at the fade out." Yet Laemmle Junior went ahead and cast her in another film, this one called *The Seed*. Bette was Margaret, ingenue daughter of John Bowles and when the *New York Times* reviewed it, they spent an entire newspaper column just trying to describe the plot. The word they eventually used was "dull". Bette herself said that the film was some sort of plea for birth control that was still too controversial a subject for Hollywood and all but got ignored in the film. "The theme and I met the same fate." Again she did not have anyone doing her make-up and no attempt was made to light her properly. When she saw the film she decided, "If I wasn't dead in pictures already, this appearance was sure to do the trick." The best thing to be said for this loser of a film is that if you are not watching too carefully, you miss Bette.

When her first three months were up, to Bette's total surprise, Universal renewed her contract. "As there wasn't the smallest doubt that I would be dropped like a hot potato, I got the shock of my life when I was called into Mr. Laemmle's office and told I was to be kept on for another three months." It was several weeks before she found out why. It seems the cameraman on *Bad Sister*, Karl Freund had saved the day by telling Laemmle, "Davis has lovely eyes."

Her next film was *Waterloo Bridge*, after a play by Robert Sherwood. The picture starred Mae Clark and Kent Douglass (who later changed his name to Douglass Montgomery, although it didn't help much). Bette played his sister, her third forgettable role. The best part of the film is the air raid sequence. Not that the acting is noteworthy, just that the studio did a fairly good job of producing an air raid.

At this point Bette's story gets slightly complicated, mainly because it's more than half a century later and no one who was involved then and still alive today seems to be able to pinpoint the exact dates. Somewhere around the end of *Waterloo Bridge*, Universal extended her contract yet again. That made a total of nine months. And at the same time, for no reason that anyone can explain, her salary was raised to $450 a week. A fourth film was slated for her but Laemmle Junior was fast coming to the conclusion that nine months was too long and $450 was too much. Mae Clark got the role that Bette would have had in *Frankenstein* because Laemmle had other plans for her. He suddenly decided to hedge his bets and rent her out to any studio who'd take her.

The first to come along was Pandro S. Berman whose company was called Radio Pictures, later to be RKO. He wanted to do a film based on the then popular radio series, *Way Back Home*. A preacher in Maine spends his time solving everybody's problems with good, old-fashioned home spun warmth. Bette played Mary Lucy, "the neighbour's daughter who helps the boy she has befriended". Another forgettable film. And *Weekly Variety* told it like it was. "As entertainment the film is unbelievably bad. The story is strictly an old-style proposed tear-jerker. It runs eighty-one minutes and seems like two-hundred and eighty-one." Nevertheless, her experience with Berman and the house that would become RKO was a good one. She wrote in her autobiography "This was the first picture in which I was well photographed, and more important, was not a sister. I was someone's girl and you did understand why he wanted to kiss me at the fade-out. When I saw the picture, I anyway, was encouraged by my physical appearance. I looked the way I had always felt I looked. For the first time. What little ego I had, had certainly taken a beating those first six months at Universal."

Her hair was ash blonde when she came to Hollywood but in comparison to the glamour girls of the day she was a brunette. For *Way Back Home* her hair was bleached very-blonde and it stayed that way for the next four years.

Columbia Pictures came along and rented her for *The Menace,* a below average melodrama adapted from an Edgar Wallace novel. It was shot in a mere eight days which tells you something about the quality of the production. Bette's achievement in the film was to scream on cue. And if this film, and Bette's acting in it, went unnoticed by everyone else, at least one of the bit players saw it differently. Murray Kinnell was his name and something about Bette impressed him.

The third of the "loan-outs" was to Capital Films for *Hell's House,* starring Pat O'Brien. The British title was *Other People's Business.* It was about juvenile delinquency, bootlegging and seventy-two minutes long. It was also almost the end of her career. One critic thought her work was "sincere" but at Universal they simply shrugged. When she came back to them after *Hell's House,* they wished her luck and announced they would not be renewing her contract this time. Suddenly she was out of work and the future didn't look very bright. With six films to her credit, there wasn't a single one that stood out as being memorable. Yet she felt she had learned a lot about the business and that each performance had shown some improvement, had brought out more confidence in her work, had made her name better known to the public. Universal obviously didn't agree and for a while it seemed as if no one in Hollywood believed in her. No one except Murray Kinnell, who just as her Universal contract was wearing down to its final hours, was singing her praises to his friend George Arliss.

As any film buff knows, Arliss was a living legend in Hollywood. He was one of the relatively few silent screen stars who managed the transition to sound. Not exactly today's stereotype of a Hollywood leading man, Arliss was even then far from what many women usually considered handsome. He had a pointed nose, didn't always stand up straight and was a bit too skinny. Yet he had a special presence that came across on the silver screen and he was very much a star. One of the problems with most silent film heroes was that their voice was either downright lousey or they had terrible diction. Arliss' voice was high pitched but less irritating than many, and his diction was far superior to most. Another problem was that many silent actors could only mime. Most of them couldn't really act. And here Arliss excelled. His extensive and impressive stage background had forged an actor with an ability that critics liked to describe as "masterful". It's recognizable even today when you see his 1929 version of *Disraeli.* He had starred in the silent version eight years previously, but when he put the character to sound, even at the age of sixty-one, you can see why Arliss was a star. In fact, the studio showed him such respect that they billed him as Mr. George Arliss, the "Mr." being an honour reserved for very, very few. He followed that success with films like *The Green Goddess* and *Old English,* classics of the genre, interestingly enough directed by Alfred E. Green who would later play a major role in Bette's career. In 1931 Arliss let John Adolphi direct him in a film adaptation of an Arliss stage triumph, *Alexander Hamilton* and that was followed by a Booth Tarkington script for a film called *The Millionaire.* They all added up to give Arliss super-star status with a heavy helping of literacy mixed in. Intelligent audiences and critics alike appreciated that an Arliss film had a strong sense of the theatre in addition to being a box office success. One of the important characteristics of his films was that he liked to populate

In Hell's House *with Pat O'Brien.*

them with actors and actresses who had legitimate stage experience. He felt it gave his films a certain sense of dignity. And that was one of the reasons why no actress in her right mind . . . especially one whose contract had just expired and who was starting to pack her bags for the trip back east . . . would turn down a part in a George Arliss film.

It was 1932. Arliss was planning to remake in sound his silent hit, *The Man Who Played God*. There was a part in the film for a young woman and Kinnell convinced Arliss that Bette Davis was just the young woman for that part.

She played Grace, the young girl infatuated with the greatness of concert pianist Montgomery Royale, played of course by Arliss. During a private concert for a European king, a bomb is hurled though a window and Royale is rendered deaf by the blast. In despair, Royale returns to America with his sister, a woman who loves him named Mildred and Grace, now his fiancée. He learns to read lips and makes a sport out of eavesdropping on other peoples' conversations when they think he is out of hearing range. One of the people he "listens" to is Grace as she informs a young man named Harold that although she is in love with him, she could never leave Royale because of his affliction. Royale, being a true hero, confronts Grace and insists she go off with Harold whilst he turns his attentions to Mildred. As the curtain comes down he has not only found true love but he is beginning to discover his music. The message is one of true happiness through good deeds. Today the film seems to border on over-simplified silliness. It has aged poorly, but at the time audiences cried and the critics raved. One of the neat gimmicks in the film, one of the few things to survive today's critical view, is Adolphi's direction, eliminating the sound whenever Royale cannot read the lips of the speaking players. The film was remade in 1955, this time starring Liberace with Dorothy Malone playing Grace. The title was *Sincerely Yours* and it's a film well worth forgetting. The reason it worked in 1932 has to be Arliss. His acting today would be considered heavy and at sixty-four he was obviously too old to play Royale but the power of his presence and the rapport he had with the audience at that time more than made up for it. His interest in Bette's career also gave her the break she needed. He saw to it that she received the proper attention by make-up specialists, hair stylists, wardrobe people and helped with the direction when he felt it was necessary. The cast, which included people like Louise Closser Hale, Donald Cook, Ray Milland and Hedda Hopper worked like a closely knit, well-disciplined stage company. They all had that same theatrical background and it showed on the set.

"Looking back over my life in Hollywood," Bette recalled at one point in the late '40s, "it is probable that *The Man Who Played God* was my most important picture. I did others that I liked better and which were far more significant but there was something about appearing as Mr. Arliss' leading lady which gave me standing."

Nicely enough, in 1977 when the American Film Institute gave her their Life Achievement Award, one of the first people she acknowledged was George Arliss. But then the Davis/Arliss respect was a two-way street. In his 1940 biography, *My Ten Years In The Studio*, Arliss left no doubt about his feelings regarding Bette's performance in *The Man Who Played God*. He wrote that he only saw certain aspects of Grace's character during rehearsals when Bette pointed them out. "I think that only two or three times in my experience have I ever got from an actor at rehearsal something beyond what I realized was in the part. Bette Davis proved to be one of these exceptions." He confided frankly that he had not been expecting anything more from her than a "nice little performance"but when they began to rehearse, "She startled me. The nice, little part became a deep and vivid creation." And finally he added, "I'm not in the least surprised that Bette Davis is now the most important star on the screen".

While a few newspaper critics felt Bette might have spoken a little too rapidly for the microphone, people in the business sat up and took notice of her performance in the film. Hal Wallis, for example, at that time one of the Warner Brothers producers, has been quoted as saying that from the time he saw Bette in *The Man Who Played God*, he knew immediately she would go all the way to the top. "She didn't just act with her eyes. She acted with her whole body . . . she jumped out of the screen."

With George Arliss in The Man Who Played God.

The Dark Horse *with Warren William.*

As soon as the picture left Hollywood to make the rounds of the nation's theatres, the first reaction to Bette's success was that the Warner Brothers picked up her contract. Jack Warner signed her on for seven years and immediately threw a handful of scripts her way. Five films were slated for her that year. Suddenly life looked a whole lot better. She felt Warners was a studio where her talents would be better used than they had been at Universal. What she didn't know then was that life at Warners would also be an uphill fight.

The first two pictures she did for them were actually filmed at the same time. *So Big* matched Bette with Barbara Stanwyck and George Brent. *The Rich Are Always With Us* teamed her with Ruth Chatterton and George Brent again.

Stanwyck was less than a year older than Bette and like her, had come to Hollywood from the East Coast with a stage background. She had been making films in California since 1929 although it would not be until well into the '30s and '40s that she would become one of the great women of the screen. Most people today, at least in the United States, think of her in the starring role in the television series *The Big Valley*, rather than for her work in such films as *Baby Face, Double Indemnity, Union Pacific, Annie Oakley, The Strange Love of Martha Ivers, Forty Guns, Walk On The Wild Side, Stella Dallas, Ball Of Fire* or *Sorry Wrong Number. So Big* was her eleventh film, but unlike Bette, Barbara Stanwyck was already a star.

Ruth Chatterton's image in those days was that of the ideal American beauty and *Vanity Fair* magazine listed her with Dietrich and Garbo. Born in New York in 1893, she died in Connecticut in 1961. By the time she and Bette worked together she had already appeared in screen hits like *Sons Of The Fathers, Madame X, Laughing Lady* and *Unfaithful.*

George Brent's career in many ways paralleled Bette's, at least for a while, because they made a total of eleven films together. Tall, dark and rugged, he was born in Dublin, Ireland in 1904. On screen he came across as a man loaded with affable self-confidence. Off screen he was known to be relatively crude. Some of his better films include *Baby Face, 42nd Street, Painted Veil, Jezebel, Dark Victory* and *Great Lie.*

Bette was first cast in *So Big*, and while working on that film, Warners put her into *The Rich Are Always With Us.* Life became hectic for her working on two films simultaneously, doing scenes for one during the day then shooting her scenes for the other at night. In *The Lonely Life* she says it was *The Rich Are Always With Us* during the day, *So Big* at night. Other accounts claim it was the other way around. What was important was that she managed to remember which role she was playing since the two were sufficiently different to have seriously got in each other's way.

In *So Big* she played Dallas O'Mara, a young artist who, by the end of the picture, saves the day. Barbara Stanwyck is Selina Peake, a school teacher in the rural midwest, with a son named Dirk. The child grows up to be something of a disappointment and Selina turns for comfort to Roelfe, played by George Brent, a successful artist. Dallas is in love with Dirk and when he brings her home to meet his mother, Dallas becomes Sellina's hope that her son, under such a good influence, will finally amount to something. The film was based on Edna Ferber's Pulitzer Prize winning novel but only ran eighty-two minutes on the screen. It was hardly long enough to do the book justice. This particular version was the second time that *So Big* had been filmed. The first was a silent version in 1925 starring Colleen Moore as Selina, and Phyllis Haver as Dallas. A third attempt was made in 1953 with Jane Wyman and Nancy Olsen.

Adequately directed by William Wellman, the film was really a Barbara Stanwyck vehicle although Bette's performance managed to sneak into the reviews. The critics called her "unusually competent".

The reviews for *The Rich Are Always With Us* weren't any better but this film did serve to further educate Bette in movie making. Ruth Chatterton played an extremely wealthy New York socialite, Caroline Van Dyke. When she confesses her marital problems to Julian, played by Brent, he confesses his love for her. The two go off together to Paris where Caroline files for divorce. Just then financial troubles befall

Caroline's husband and she is concerned for him. Julian becomes annoyed and returns to New York. She follows him but finds that he has not been waiting for her. Instead he's been running around with Malbro, played by Bette. Love overcomes jealousy and Julian returns to Caroline.

It was an attempt at high comedy by director Alfred E. Green, but he didn't pull it off very well. The papers said it was "mildly diverting" giving Ruth Chatterton her usual "charming" ratings. All they basically said about Bette was that she "served well".

A few important things, however, stand out about this film. Firstly, there is the "cigarette scene". Brent puts two cigarettes into his mouth and lights them both at the same time. It was used again in *Now, Voyager*. Secondly, Bette learned a few things through her relationship with Ruth Chatterton. Bette had admittedly been quite nervous about working with such a star and Ruth Chatterton really did have quite a bit of magic about her both on the screen and off. The first day of shooting, Ruth Chatterton arrived on the set literally sweeping through the doors with movie-star authority. Bette was dazzled. She found her regal and superb, even the way she chewed gum. Unfortunately though, it only added to the nervousness Bette already felt about working with her. It all came to a head during a slightly awkward few seconds when they did their first scene together. It was inside a restaurant where Brent was sitting at a table with Ruth Chatterton. Bette was to walk over and say hello. As Bette told it, "I was actually so terrified of her I literally could not get a word out of my mouth". She said that Ruth Chatterton sat there looking at her in a superior kind of way until Bette inadvertantly let go with, "I'm so damned scared of you, I'm speechless". That broke the ice and Bette later remembered, "She was most helpful in her scenes with me after that. I never forgot this experience and in later years, when young actors were terrified of me, I would always try to help them get over it".

There is also a fairly classic Bette Davis line in the film. Malbro asks Caroline, "What's a girl to do when she's terribly in love with a man and he won't take her seriously?" It's a line she delivers with darting eyes. And while it would still take a lot of years and a lot of films to make lines and eyes like that famous, by 1932 Bette was at least on her way.

Alfred E. Green directed Bette again in her next picture, *The Dark Horse*. It's a satire on political campaigns. *Photoplay Magazine* promised the film would "Give you enough chuckles to tide you over a flock of gloomy days". *Photoplay Magazine* also exaggerated, although the film still has a few amusing moments. More importantly, it was Bette's first film as the true leading lady. The problem was that *Dark Horse* was a typical "B" picture, the kind of product that the Warners ground out on a well-oiled assembly line. This one was done so fast they didn't even have time for a lot of close-ups. By the way, the film was based on an original story by someone named Melville Crossman. You can learn a lot about how Warner Brothers operated in those days when you find out that Melville Crossman was the *nom de plume* for the studio's production boss, Darryl Zanuck.

To plug *Dark Horse*, Bette and her leading man Warren William went on a tour of the country. It paved the way with the movie-going public for her next film, *Cabin In The Cotton*, one of the films that helped to make her a real star. Zanuck insisted that the role of Madge was right for her. The picture's director Michael Curtiz was not so happy. He supposedly put up quite a fight to keep her off the film but Zanuck had his way. Richard Barthelmess, one of the many silent screen stars who hadn't translated well into sound, had his last major role in this film. He played Marvin, a sharecropper's son who falls for the vixen, Madge. It's the story of sharecroppers versus plantation owners and just to set the record straight, at the beginning of the film there is a disclaimer on behalf of the Warners saying that it is not their intention to take sides in the sharecropper/plantation owner dispute. They said they were merely trying to show the conditions that existed. While much of the action revolves around Marvin's ambitions and his poor boy's honesty, the picture is very much a period piece because whatever that sharecropper/plantation owner controversy was then, it isn't now.

A first rate acting job by Bette is what comes across these days. She vindicated Zanuck's faith in her and managed to pull it off. No thanks though to Curtiz who made life as tough for her as he could. No thanks either to Barthelmess who proved he was long past his best. Off screen he was easy going and kindly but on the screen he comes across as expressionless and wooden. She also found his technique baffling. He did no acting in the long shots, only slightly more in the medium shots and, for the most part, overacted in the close-ups. Bette wasn't actually the female lead in this film . . . Dorothy Jordan had that honour . . . but in one scene Bette sang, and throughout the others she had the best of the lines. Some of those lines really have become Bette Davis classics. For example, in one scene, with full southern drawl, she says to Barthelmess, "You don't like me, do ya?" He answers, "I do." And she says, "Then come close, I won't bite ya." In another she cuts into the action with a lazy, "Sorry to interrupt ya little *tête-à-tête*". Seducing Barthelmess, she lures him to her room, then instructs him to, "Turn ya back while I get in to something restful." But the line she really scored with is one of her all-time favourites. "Ah'd love to kiss ya, but I just washed ma hay-uh!"

Madge was by far her meatiest role to date and probably her best acting job as well. Until Madge, she simply didn't have the characters to work with. This time she proved herself by playing the sexy bitch with such conviction that the New York *Herald Tribune* said "The girl is superb."

It was the first step in what would prove to be the proper road to stardom. As she herself put it, "Madge in *Cabin In The Cotton* was my first downright, forthright bitch and one would have thought that the role would have erased permanently the sweet, drab sister type that had plagued me since my arrival".

Surprisingly, however, it didn't.

The Cabin In The Cotton *with Richard Barthelmess.*

In The Rich Are Always With Us.

Fighting for Stardom

IN A LOT OF WAYS, the 1930s were strange times. Warners, like other studios, was pounding out films much the same way factories all over the world churned out their products. In 1932 alone Warners produced fifty-seven films. The following year they made fifty-two films. That meant one hundred and nine movies in just one hundred and four weeks. It was the start of those "Golden Days" of the studio system where the production boss was God and the actors were under contract as if the studio were nothing more than a big repertory company. The rules of the game were no more complicated than this. Put your actors on to a sound stage, tell them what to do, get it all on film, get the film out to the movie houses and go on to the next film. If you hit, you made money. If you didn't, you tried to make up your losses with your next hit. What your actors might have to say about anything was really inconsequential. The important thing was volume.

For the Warner Brothers and their accountants, it hardly mattered that some of the stars might not like their make-up or, that some of their directors couldn't help a star understand the motivation for a scene. Make-up was supposed to make you look beautiful in front of the camera and motivation for any scene was your weekly salary cheque. Having anything to do with actors, except putting them in front of a camera, was not how the studio paid its bills. And by the middle of 1932, Jack Warner and Darryl Zanuck actually went on record as saying that all actors were, in effect, a pain in the neck. Of course, at the time there wasn't any way of making movies without them . . . it was Disney who eventually figured that one out with full-length animation . . . so they did what they thought might be the next best thing. They told actors that whatever their opinions were about anything, these opinions should be forgotten. In a statement issued July 25th, signed by Warner and Zanuck, everyone on the lot was informed that no artist under contract to the studio would be given any say whatsoever in any respect of any film production. Full stop!

It was no small wonder then that neither Warner nor Zanuck particularly cared to hear what Bette Davis had to say when, after her success in *Cabin In The Cotton*, she found herself playing Ruth in a tiresome film called *Three On A Match*. The Warners had proved themselves so sensitive to both her career and her acting ability, that they had shoved her right back into a true-blue sweetheart role.

Ann Dvorak played the socialite. Joan Blondell was the showgirl. Bette was stuck with the part of the secretary. Bogart was somewhere in the cast and so was Lyle Talbot and the storyline had to do with the lives of the three girls who grew up together, were separated by circumstances and come back to talk about their lives a dozen years later. Mervyn Leroy, a Warner son-in-law with no real talent as a director, found he could get away with substituting pace for style. He also won Bette's heart by criticizing her acting ability and making a point of telling her that she'd never go very far. It seems he preferred singing the praises of Joan Blondell instead. The premise of the film revolves around the war-time superstition that it was unlucky to be the third person lighting a cigarette from the same match. It turns out to be a very weak premise, even if it lasted only sixty-three minutes. Strangely enough, however, the reviews were mixed. A hard thing to believe half a century later as you fight to stay awake during the film. The *New York Times* labelled the whole affair "tedious and distasteful". Yet *Hollywood Filmograph* thought *Three On A Match* was "hard hitting, fast melodrama, handled with real motion picture intelligence. It was well acted and Mervyn Leroy's direction is excellent". Then they added, "Bette Davis was ravishing in appearance but had very little to do". Years later, in spite of the compliment

Caught back of the camera in an off-stage moment during the shooting of Housewife.

about her looks, Bette said she had to agree with the *New York Times* review.

By the time the film was finished, she found herself scheduled to act with James Cagney who was by this time very much a star at Warners. A Broadway veteran, he debuted in Hollywood with *Sinner's Holiday*, a 1930 screen version of the play in which he had starred in New York. That was followed by *Doorway To Hell* (released in the UK as *A Handful of Clouds*). There was a "working man's drama" called *Other Men's Women* and then one of his all-time greats, the one which made him a star, *The Public Enemy*. (The British title was *Enemies Of The Public*.) The moment Cagney stuffed that grapefruit in Mae Clarke's face, his career took off. Two years and a bunch of films later, he and Bette were going to work together but the Warner edict of July 25th didn't sit well with him. He figured he had enough weight to fight back and he did. The studio was supposedly losing money during the Depression . . . Warner accountants reported the net loss for 1932 was in excess of $14 million . . . but Cagney couldn't see how this was his problem. To keep those losses from climbing higher, Jack Warner ordered pay cuts for everyone. They ranged from twenty to fifty per cent. Cagney found himself making only $1000 a week although some reports put the figure above that. Whatever it actually was, it meant that he was making less than he was used to even though these were the days of nickel apples and quarter lunches. He just wasn't going to stand for it. Joan Blondell, who had worked with him in a bunch of films, was making a mere $250 a week and Bette probably wasn't now getting much more. But Cagney felt he was Cagney, so he walked out. He came back only when the Academy of Arts and Sciences decided that his salary should be raised to $1750 a week.

In the meantime, he missed out playing Tom Connors to Bette's Fay in the Michael Curtiz film *20,000 Years In Sing Sing*. Bette would have to wait to work with Cagney. In this film the Cagney role went to a young actor Warners somehow managed to borrow from the Fox Studios . . . his name was Spencer Tracy.

Except for a radio show years later, this was the only time Bette and Tracy ever worked together. Bette has often said she's always regretted not having been able to work with him again and according to at least one Tracy biographer, he felt the same way. They had known each other in New York, both had stage backgrounds, they shared a birthday and they enjoyed working together. In *20,000 Years In Sing Sing* Bette and Tracy were teamed against director Michael Curtiz whom Bette must have figured would simply repeat his performances of harrassment. Tracy then became not only an actor to work with but something of an ally. This time around, however, Curtiz ran slightly less true to form. He obviously felt that *20,000 Years In Sing Sing* was a man's picture so he didn't have to bother with Bette. He played most of the film off Tracy. He used a semi-documentary style that gives the picture that kind of harsh edge that prison flicks then always seemed to have. Lots of shadows. Clanking metal. Both at the beginning and at the end he superimposes on each man passing in front of the camera the length of his prison term. Ten years. Seventy-five years. One year. Five years. The script was loosely based on the autobiography of Lewis Lawes, a former Sing Sing warden. Lawes himself was actually involved with the production of the film and his technical advice, combined with Curtiz's macho instincts, is good enough to convince you that the whole thing was filmed at Sing Sing instead of on a Hollywood lot. The 20,000 years in the title refers to the total time being served by all the inmates. Tracy's Tom Connors was only supposed to be there for five to thirty years but when Bette, as his moll Fay, kills Joe Finn, played by Louis Calhern, Tracy admits to the killing and gets "the chair". Bette plays with her usual intensity and Tracy is simply Tracy. The talent is already obvious and you can't help but know that by this time he was well on his way to being a star. With Bette it's not quite as evident mainly because Curtiz managed to hide a lot of it behind Tracy. At one point where Tracy is given leave from prison to visit her on what everyone thinks is her death bed, Curtiz placed the camera so that Tracy is handsomely framed while all you see of Bette is her nostrils. Yet Tracy himself recognized talent when he saw it and supposedly asked for Bette when Jack Warner hired him for the film. Tracy had seen *Hell's House* and was fascinated by her unpredictable gaiety. He reportedly said to her "You could be the best actress in pictures today. I'll correct that. You are the most talented."

One interesting footnote to *20,000 Years In Sing Sing* is that this is one of those films that didn't quite make it although it set a certain standard as a tough, no nonsense kind of prison film, with the compassionate and understanding warden. In this version the warden was played by Arthur Byron. But in 1940 the script was reworked and shot as *Castle On The Hudson* with Pat O'Brien playing the warden, one of the best roles of his career.

Bette approached the picture with hope for a role in which she could excel. She came out of it disappointed in many ways. As she wrote in *The Lonely Life*, "I had daydreams about the Director with Vision who would see what I knew I had. I rudely woke up to find myself cast in a Michael Curtiz picture." But then she said, "I was good as the moll and my notices made that clear." However, the Brothers Warner didn't seem to read the notices. "My reward was a little epic called *Parachute Jumper*, opposite young Fairbanks, the Crown Prince of Hollywood, scion of Pickfair and consort to MGM's Princess Royal, Joan of Crawford. Doug was already saying 'profeel' for one's side view which goes to prove that people do not change, simply develop and grow. I was again a secretary . . . Warners were vaguely aware, evidently, of a possible niche for me. It took patience on my part."

Bette played the southern girl named Alabama . . . it was the second time she had a role with that name, almost as if all southern girls had to be called that, the way everyone from Texas was always Tex . . . and Fairbanks was Bill, the handsome pilot. Leo G. Carroll was Weber, a slick character who hires Bill first as a body guard, then as a smuggler. Directed by Alfred E. Green, the film tended, as one critic described it, make better use out of stock aerial footage for the flying scenes than it did out of the script. If nothing else, Bette had a chance to use her southern accent again, Fairbank's moved on to swashbuckling and Leo G. Carroll turned up years later as Topper on television.

By this time Bette had heard about *Of Human Bondage*. She also knew that better scripts existed than *Parachute Jumper* and if she was ever going to do anything at all with her career, she'd have to make a stand. It was very obvious to her that no one was going to hand her anything on a silver platter and proof of that came when she saw the next film Warners had in store for her. It was called *The Mind Reader* starring Warren William and directed by Roy Del Ruth. The script struck her as so mindless that she put her foot down. She fought and she argued and she simply refused to do it. And for the first time she managed to make her point clear enough for Jack Warner and Darryl Zanuck to understand. They backed down and let her off the film. It wasn't a big point to win but it was nevertheless a victory and there was a lesson to be learned from it. If she screamed loud enough and long enough she could do fair battle.

But it was not a victory without casualties. She was taken off the picture and her satisfaction was quickly replaced by the nightmare all actors share . . . that there wouldn't be another picture.

Constance Cummings took the role that was to have been Bette's . . . *The Mind Reader* didn't do much for her career either . . . and there sat Bette without a script. It was in many ways, a repeat of her last days at Universal. Insecurity gripped her and she began worrying about it being the end of her career. But just like those last days at Universal, it was George Arliss who appeared on cue. He wanted her for *The Working Man*, a film that can't be described in any other way than pure escapism in the classic '30s tradition. Arliss, playing a shoe manufacturer named Reeves leaves his business to his nephew and goes off on a fishing vacation to Maine. There he meets a young man named Tommy, played by Theodore Newton and Tommy's sister Jenny, played by Bette. The script notes describe Jenny's character as "directionless". As it happens, Tommy and Jenny are the children of another shoe manufacturer who, as fate has it, is Reeves' most important competitor. Seeing a chance to amuse himself, Reeves tells Tommy that he is out of work because of the Depression. So Tommy hires him to work in the shoe factory which Reeves reorganizes, going into competition with his own nephew, who in the meantime has been wondering why the fishing trip is taking so long. The whole thing is so totally ridiculous that it would hardly be worth seeing today except for the fact that director John Adolfi knowingly shot it tongue in cheek so it still retains a little of its humour. It looks like an early TV sit-com and comes off as a classic example of what might be termed "Depression day comedy". In any case, unlike a lot of the films she did before, this one certainly didn't hurt her career. *Film Daily* thought "Bette Davis scores strong", and she did too in Jack Warner's mind. From this point on, he decided, she would be a star. "It was the first important picture I had made in ages," she later wrote. "After a few days of shooting, my mentor (George Arliss) smiled that wise smile and said, 'My little girl isn't afraid of me anymore, is she?'"

Hardly. Arliss' 'little girl' was now a veteran of fifteen films. "On my first picture with him," she remembered in her autobiography, "I expected everyday that the axe would fall." Although she immediately added that Arliss himself never gave her reason to believe that and was always 'a lamb'. "But," she said, "his talent was so impressive that the young actor quaked. It is amazing that when one arrives and is elevated to true stardom, he may be the same human being but he is an ogre to the rest of the cast who now imagine they are in the presence of Ghenghis Khan."

Arliss, of course, was not alone in affecting her that way. So did Ruth Chatterton when they first worked together. In later years Bette herself affected many younger actors the same way. For example, in 1980 Bette did a film for American television called *Skyward*, directed by Ron Howard who grew up on TV first as Opie, in *The Andy Griffith Show*, and then as Richie, friend of the Fonz in *Happy Days*. This was the fourth film he had directed but he had never worked with a star like Bette Davis. As he told *The Washington Post* in an interview, "Most directors work all their lives and never work with Bette Davis, and here's little Opie." Bette played an ex-stunt pilot in the film and got the part because Howard and producer Anson Williams, also an acting veteran from *Happy Days,* had heard Bette say in an interview that she was tired of playing "crusty old lady" parts. "I think she was a little dubious," Howard told the interviewer Carla Hall. "She kept calling me Mr. Howard. She knew how old I was."

If Bette's attitude made Howard quake the way Bette did when she first dealt with Arliss, it certainly wasn't an intentional psychological game she was playing. As she told Carla Hall, 'I had enormous qualms. This is the first time in years I haven't had director approval. I just decided to do it. Over the phone I was very rude to Ron Howard. I couldn't imagine this kid directing."

As it turned out, once she saw that Howard had talent, whatever tensions might have existed faded away. One day after shooting she slapped him on the bottom and said, "Okay Ron, see you tomorrow." As he explained it, "From that point on, I'd gained her confidence."

And perhaps confidence is the key word. If Arliss made her quake in the beginning, it likely had to do with her own lack of confidence in being able to live up to his expectations and being able to hold her own in scenes with him. The same went for Ruth Chatterton whose "star-like" style of walking on to a set threw Bette totally off balance. But with each film she gained more confidence and by the time she and Arliss made *The Working Man*, although she says she was still very impressed with him as an actor, she was no longer personally afraid of him. "I was growing up," she said years later. "He was delighted. He taught me always to think of what came before a scene and what was about to come after. Scenes being shot out of sequence are the devil to play." But in this film she had twice as much experience as she did when she made *The Man Who Played God* and it showed on screen. "*The Working Man* was another big success," she said, "and dignified my struggle to the point where Darryl Zanuck decided it was time to give me the glamour-star treatment. It was a great mistake. I wasn't the type to be glamorized in the usual way. In an ecstacy of poor taste and a burst of misspent energy, I was made over and cast as the star of a piece of junk called *Ex-Lady*."

A remake of Barbara Stanwyck's *Illicit,* this was the first time Bette's name was above the titles, a sure sign of star-status in Hollywood. In this case, however, it was an honour she probably could have done without. *Ex-Lady* is the story of Helen, a woman ahead of her time because she believes in living with the man she loves instead of marrying him. In those days this was pretty provocative stuff. Gene Raymond played her live-in friend. All is well until he insists they get married, at which point the relationship takes a nose-dive. So does the advertising business they have worked to make a success. The suggestion is that Helen feels marriage is too confining an institution for intelligent, creative adults. As their friendship falls apart, she accuses him of having an affair . . . which drives him out of their apartment . . . and then he accuses her of having an affair, which finally drives the audience to sleep. In the end it turns out that they are both innocent of wrong-doings and in honour of the great American dream she agrees to give the idea of marriage one more chance. Hopefully they lived happily ever after. Luckily Bette made a bunch of better films.

Film Daily wrote: "Some fairly hot scenes are sprinkled here and there but the story in general has no guts and the arguments for love without marriage are never very convincing or as shocking as intended."

The *New York Times* wrote: "Bette Davis, a young actress who has shown intelligence in the roles assigned to her in films, has had the misfortune to be cast in the principal role of *Ex-Lady.* What the somewhat sinister event meant to her employers was that Miss Davis, having shown herself to be possessed of the proper talent and pictorial allure, now became a star in her own right. What it meant to her embarrassed admirers . . . was that Miss Davis had to spend an uncomfortable amount of time *en deshabille* in boudoir scenes, engaged in repartee and in behaviour which were sometimes timidly suggestive, then depressively naïve and mostly downright foolish."

And in *The Lonely Life,* Bette herself wrote best of all. "It is a part of my career that my unconscious tastefully avoids. I only recall that from the daily shooting to the billboards, falsely picturing me half-naked, my shame was only exceeded by my fury."

Quite happily, she grabbed at her next script. Anything had to be better than the excrutiatingly bad *Ex-Lady.* So the general silliness of *Bureau Of Missing Persons* must have been a relief. Co-starring Pat O'Brien, Lewis Stone and Glenda Farrell, under the direction of Roy Del Ruth, it's one of those little comedies that used to be called "fast moving" as an excuse by critics or publicity men for a story with a lot of action but little credibility. Bette plays a suspected murderess and Pat O'Brien has forty-eight hours to track her down. As time runs out he borrows a corpse from the local morgue . . . which in itself is rather funny . . . and buries it in Bette's name. Of course, it's just a ploy to get her to come to the funeral and when she shows up, he nabs her . . . except now there's someone's twin brother who also shows up and he turns out to be the real killer. It was probably a lot easier to accept such things in those days.

As 1933 came to an end, Bette and William Powell were part of the cast assembled by William Dieterle for *Fashions Of 1934* which was released during the first couple of weeks of January. Powell plays a businessman who manages to convince Bette, a fashion designer, that there is a lot of money to be made in copying exclusive Parisian fashions which can be sold in America undercutting French prices. Somehow they find themselves in Paris trying to steal designs but when the *haute couture* houses prove too smart for them, Powell goes into show business, which is how Busby Berkeley came to be involved. After all, there had to be something in the plot of the film to explain all those dancing ladies!

Throughout the picture Bette sports a platinum wig, false eyelashes and slinky clothes. Even if in their hearts they knew better, the Warners just kept on trying to turn Bette into another Greta Garbo.

Costumes for *Fashions of 1934* were designed by Orry-Kelly, one of the all-time great costume designers in the history of motion pictures and Bette worked with him in nearly twenty films.

Born without the hyphen, he was hired by Warners as Jack Kelly in the very early '30s. It was a team of Warner studio publicity men who put the hyphen there to make his act sound a little sexier. The business of wardrobe in those days wasn't what it is today. Orry-Kelly was hired only after several years of freelance costume designing for Barbara Stanwyck and Ruth Chatterton. Until he came along, it seems that none of the other studios had designers on their staff. Once he was on salary, most of the other studios also hired designers. Orry-Kelly first dressed Bette in *The Man Who Played God* because George Arliss insisted that she be well dressed. In *20,000 Years In Sing Sing* Orry-Kelly designed clothes for her so chicly that in the scene where she first visits Tracy in prison, he tells her not to wear such clothes because she looks too terrific. The next visit she's dressed in a very sober suit, complete with a necktie and hat, and this time Tracy wonders, "Where's your cigar?" Orry-Kelly's contribution to *Ex-Lady* was mostly nightgowns and lace underwear, much to Bette's chagrin but he made up for it by giving her fabulously sequinned gowns to wear in *Bordertown*. For *Dangerous* he put her in a series of dresses and blouses that changed in style to show how the heroine's success changed throughout the film. Then came the famous strapless red gown that he made for Bette in *Jezebel*. It was a catalyst for much of the action in the film, and had this been a stage production, the dress would have had to be red. But costumes for film are different from costumes for the stage and Orry-Kelly knew that deep rust would show up on a black and white screen looking actually more like red. In other words, the famous red dress wasn't really red. *Time Magazine* did a cover story on Bette in their March 28, 1938 issue but the picture shows her in a gown that was only used in the tests, never the film.

Orry-Kelly played with colour again in designing costumes for Bette in *Juarez*. She is the Empress Carlotta who gradually goes insane. He helped in making the progression to madness more believable by starting her off in a white dress, then greying her clothes at each step until she finally goes off the deep end, dressed in black.

He designed Victorian costumes for *The Old Maid* and Elizabethan ones for *The Private Lives of Elizabeth and Essex*. For that film he and Bette spent an entire week going over reference books to make certain that her clothes were absolutely correct. Then it seems he had to do two sets of costumes for her . . . one for the tests and one for the actual shootings . . . because Michael Curtiz insisted on certain costume changes and Bette wouldn't have anything less than historically accurate costumes.

By this time, Orry-Kelly was very much a star in his own right, perhaps not with the general public, but certainly with everyone on the Warners lot. Costumes were now an integral part of every film. In pictures like *The Sisters*, he was called on to do nearly three dozen costumes and given a budget of almost $1000 per costume, then an enormous sum. He dressed Bette in *The Letter, The Great Lie, The Little Foxes* and *Watch on the Rhine*. He made a couple of dozen costumes for her in *Now, Voyager* which were aimed at bringing out the shyness of the character she played. For the opening scenes of *Old Acquaintance* he put her in the top half of a man's pyjamas and as Bette explained in *Mother Goddam*, "This was a first. It resulted in quite a vogue for young girls at that time".

While it seems they might have quarrelled from time to time about costumes . . . they certainly did for *In This Our Life* . . . Orry-Kelly was still the one she trusted most for costumes and it would be hard to say that he ever let her down. In *Mr. Skeffington* he was faced with the problem of designing clothes for her that spanned twenty-six years of her life and the result was forty different costumes.

In 1943, much to everyone's shock, Orry-Kelly at the age of forty-one, got himself drafted into the army. Bette, again in *Mother Goddam*, was very frank when she said, "Warner Brothers for me without Orry-Kelly was as if I had lost my right arm. His contribution to my career was an enormous one. He never featured his clothes to such a degree that the performance was overshadowed. His clothes for *Mr. Skeffington*, his absolute dedication to what was the style of the day, was in my opinion, the greatest of all the wardrobes he designed for me."

Within a year he was back from the war but he didn't get along as well as he had with

Her only picture with Spencer Tracy –
20,000 Years In Sing Sing.

The Working Man *with George Arliss.*

Jack Warner, and Zanuck was now over at 20th Century Fox offering him more money to work there. Yet when it came time for Bette to do *The Corn Is Green* she insisted that Orry-Kelly be the one to design her costumes. She carried enough weight at the studio that he was brought back temporarily for that film. By the late '40s Warners had hired Edith Head to run their costume department, and she too became something of a wardrobe legend. But as far as Bette was concerned, she "desperately missed Orry-Kelly". The expression she used often was that she needed him "to help" her with her films. And when she needed someone "to help" in 1960 with a pair of gowns for her stage performance in *The World Of Carl Sandburg*, she turned again to Orry-Kelly. Twenty-eight years later, she was still depending on him.

The Year of Changes

IT WAS 1934. ROOSEVELT was halfway through his first term as President of the United States. MacDonald was Prime Minister of England. A World War was on its way, but if news of the coming war had filtered all the way out to Hollywood, it still wasn't something to concern the moguls. They were interested only in turning out films at a furious pace. It was just five years since the Wall Street Crash and the thought of selling apples on a street corner was enough to frighten the studio bosses into working overtime. The public wanted movies, there was money in movies and money meant you'd never have to sell apples. It might very well have been the height of Hollywood's greatest era.

Bette churned out six films that year because now there was money to be made with her name. There were eight Bette Davis films released in 1932 which was her most productive year, and after 1934 she never again did more than five in any one year. Most years she did three or less. The first of her 1934 crop was *The Big Shakedown* which brought her together with Charles Farrell, the archetypal romantic boy-next-door and Ricardo Cortez, the archetypal Latin gangster. Bette played Norma, the archetypal good girl who always wants to do the right thing. The film is an archetypal bore.

With Prohibition repealed, the bad guy Barnes is out of work. Bootleggers had to find other products to sell so Barnes manages to lure the good guy Jimmy into a business venture. Jimmy is a pharmacist and Barnes convinces him that the two of them should go into the counterfeit medicine line. His argument is that poor people who need expensive drugs could now afford them. Jimmy thinks helping the poor is a decent pursuit, all the more so when Barnes tells him that there will be enough money for him to go ahead and marry his sweetheart, Norma. Of course, these cut-rate drugs don't work because they're not the real thing and Jimmy soon sees he's about to get into trouble. Once they're married, Norma tries to talk Jimmy out of the scheme but once in with the mob it is difficult to escape. Then Norma gets pregnant and instantly has a baby. (Hollywood always has been a magical world.) Complications arise, however, and the baby needs medication. The counterfeit drugs are used and the baby dies. Jimmy disposes of Barnes in a vat of acid then confesses his crimes. The understanding police exonerate him.

Because Bette was now considered a star, the studio provided a stand-in for her. A girl named Sally Sage was hired to take over a lot of the less exciting chores that non-stars had to suffer. Sally Sage stood under the lights until the lighting director got them right. Sally Sage walked through some scenes until the film director had the blocking right. Sally Sage read lines to other actors until they had them right. Sally Sage never became a star . . . although in Hollywood any actress who's working, even as a stand-in, is better off than most. In all, she worked on a total of thirty-seven films for Bette.

While doing *The Big Shakedown*, the studio sent Bette a script to read for her next role which she immediately turned down. Warner let her get away with it and gave the role to Mary Astor. The film was called *The Case Of The Howling Dog* and was the first of many Perry Mason films.

She did accept the next offering, a James Cagney film called *Jimmy The Gent*. She probably would have been better off with Perry Mason because *Jimmy The Gent* was tailored to Cagney. He played Jimmy, she played Joan and it all has to do with some sort of harmless scheme where Jimmy makes money locating people who have recently inherited money from long-lost relatives. Joan thinks it's a racket, insists he go straight and when Jimmy says no, she falls for a slick character named Wallington, portrayed by Alan

Bette c. 1934.

Dinehart, whose most notable trait is his impeccable manners. To win back his girl, Jimmy imitates Wallington's manners and solves a crime . . . yes, somewhere in all of this there was a crime . . . and that's enough to make him a hero. Wallington is shown to be a scoundrel, Jimmy promises to go straight and Joan finds true love with him. *Variety* wrote at the time that this film was especially worthwhile for "Fans that want entertainment and don't care much about cinematic art . . ." They also had nice things to say about "Bette Davis' unusual coiffure".

Not what anyone would bother to call a great film, *Jimmy The Gent* was Bette's third picture with Michael Curtiz as director. *Cabin In The Cotton* was the first then came *20,000 Years In Sing Sing*. Like her, he too was under contract to the Brothers Warner and had little, if anything, to say about which films he directed or who would play in them. Born in Hungary, he was a former circus acrobat who constantly called everyone "You bum" instead of using a name. For understandable reasons, he was generally considered to be an unlikable guy. On top of that he had a reputation as a slave driver. He didn't want his actors to break for lunch or to stop at the end of the day. He could see no reason why they shouldn't work on right through the night. There were even instances when he got so annoyed at members of the crew that he not only insulted them verbally but also got into fist fights with them.

On a movie set today he would be considered a joke, a parody of film directors from the '30s. But in those days the riding breeches he always wore and the riding crop he always carried were considered signs of his authority and artistry. He must have gotten along with some people at Warners and Joan Blondell seems to have been one of them. One of the few perhaps, but one nevertheless, even though she eventually came to refer to him as "Crazy Mike Curtiz". He did not, however, get along with Bette and he tended, at least for the first bunch of films they did together, to make her life on the set fairly miserable. She didn't care much for him either understandably when you find out that he openly referred to her as "A no good sexless son of a bitch".

Yet to set the record straight, the Curtiz method of direction . . . the director as total fascist dictator . . . was one method that sometimes worked. *Cabin In The Cotton* was Bette's best performance up till then and he got another acting job out of her in *20,000 Years in Sing Sing*, good enough for her to hold her own with Tracy. He did the same with her role opposite Cagney. They weren't great films by today's standards and they weren't award winning performances when judged in the context of some of Bette's later work but, he got her to work like a professional and as long as she was working, she was learning. The Curtiz method worked especially well with macho stars like Cagney and Bogart. After all, it was Curtiz who did *Casablanca* which won him the Academy Award for Best Director in 1943 and *Yankee Doodle Dandy* which won Cagney the Best Actor Award in 1942.

Hired by Warners in 1926, Curtiz's first effort was a silent film called *The Third Degree*. Two years later he directed *Tenderloin* which was billed, at least by the Warner PR people, as the first actual talking picture. Two years after that he directed Al Jolson in *Mammy* which is worth remembering because it gave the world the song "Yes, We Have No Bananas". Curtiz had a magic touch when it came to dealing with Errol Flynn although the two supposedly didn't get along on a personal basis. He directed Flynn in *Captain Blood, Charge Of The Light Brigade* . . . according to legend it was during the shooting of this film that Curtiz screamed the order, "Bring on the empty horses" . . . and the 1938 version of *The Adventures of Robin Hood*. Added to the Curtiz list of great hits is *The Walking Dead* with Boris Karloff; *The Sea Wolf* with Edward G. Robinson; *Life With Father* starring William Powell and Irene Dunne; *Young Man With A Horn* (The British title was *Young Man Of Music*) with Kirk Douglas and the Ernest Hemingway story *Breaking Point* starring John Garfield. Curtiz died in 1962, having done more than eighty films for Warners.

His fourth collaboration with Bette was called *Front Page Woman*, a comedy that wasn't much better than *Jimmy The Gent*. Then they did *Kid Galahad*. Curtiz put Bette into the ring with Edward G. Robinson and Humphrey Bogart and it remains, even today, one of the all-time great boxing films. Remade a number of times . . . there is even one that starred Elvis Presley . . . the Curtiz version is a classic. It is also by far the best of the Davis/Curtiz efforts. By the time they got around to this film, even if there was still not a lot of love lost between them, they at least respected one other. She had thirty-two films worth of experience to draw on and a rough and tumble boxing film was right up Curtiz's alley. In fact, when it came time to show "the bums" exactly what he wanted, he'd get into the scene and throw punches with them.

The final film Bette did with Curtiz was *The Private Lives Of Elizabeth and Essex*, co-starring Errol Flynn and Olivia de Havilland. Bette played a woman more than twice her age and played the part very well. One reason might be that Curtiz knew all along how to get a convincing performance out of her.

The next film Bette made was *Fog Over Frisco* and with it came a different style of director. His name was William Dieterle. He and Bette had worked together for the first time on *Fashions Of 1934*. While she was less emotional about him than Curtiz, she didn't necessarily care for him either. She found him pompous and she criticized him for being pedantic. They teamed up again for *Satan Met A Lady* (which Bogart and director John Huston eventually remade into *The Maltese Falcon*) and *Juarez*. Based on her performances in those two films, Dieterle must also have understood that Bette had a talent to be exploited. Unfortunately he didn't manage to use a lot of it in *Fog Over Frisco*.

She played Arlene, a woman who hangs out in all the wrong places with all the wrong people. Her friend Val, played by Margaret Lindsay, takes on the job of defending Arlene's reputation. There are also shady goings-on with the mob who kidnaps Val, there are shoot-outs, Lyle Talbot wears his dinner jacket while pouring champagne, Donald Woods saves the day and Bette moves on to her next project.

This was her twenty-first film and it might be fair to say that by now she had paid her dues. Her name was known. She could tell the difference between a good script and a bad one and was also keenly aware of where her career stood. She was at a crossroads. Those last three films . . . *The Big Shakedown, Jimmy The Gent* and *Fog Over Frisco* hadn't advanced her career. In interviews many years later she candidly admitted that this particular period was one when she was frightened that she would be stuck in mediocre films or even see her Hollywood career come to a complete stop. She was bright enough and filled with enough good sense to understand that if she didn't come up with a big winner soon . . . not simply a good script, but a very big film . . . she might be sentenced to spend the rest of her career with films such as those last three. But by this time she had heard about *Of Human Bondage*.

Somewhere around the end of 1933 she was told that RKO was planning a film version of Somerset Maugham's story and that her name had been mentioned for the role of Mildred. Right away she knew this could be her break. John Cromwell was scheduled to direct the film but Bette was very much under contract to Jack Warner. Cromwell supposedly wanted her for the picture and Maugham himself agreed that she would be a good choice. She grew desperate. Jack Warner, however, wasn't quite as agreeable. As far as he was concerned, he owned Bette Davis and that was that.

Pandro Berman was still boss at RKO and Bette had fond memories of working with him in 1931. So she went to see him, hoping he might be able to pull some strings with Warners. He needed no convincing that she would be right for the role of Mildred although to be totally fair he tried in his own way to talk her out of it.

In those days Holywood stars were always supposed to look like Hollywood stars. Bette once described herself as the first actress in Hollywood to come out of the water looking wet. Until her, she believed, no matter what the character was, Hollywood actresses always had every hair in place. But Bette knew what she looked like and had always claimed that she wasn't pretty by Hollywood standards and that she didn't have the face of a Hollywood glamour girl no matter how much make-up was layered on. She also believed that the part of Mildred should not be played by a glamour girl because Mildred herself wasn't one. She was, Bette felt, probably very much like herself. Berman argued that the role of Mildred was not the open door to success and that many other actresses in Hollywood had shied away from the part because

Mildred was, among other things, a vicious woman. Playing such a role, Berman explained, could actually ruin a glamour-linked career. But Bette was not to be talked out of this one. For her this was not just any role. This was . . . and she was convinced of it . . . a chance in a life-time. No matter what she, knew she absolutely had to get the part.

Again, it was Jack Warner who held the veto.

As she put it in her autobiography, "John Cromwell wanted me for the part . . . After seeing me in *Cabin In The Cotton* and *The Rich Are Always With Us* he felt I could do justice to the role. Besides, as a heroine she was such a disagreeable character no well-established actress would play her. The picture was to star Leslie Howard. I told Mr. Cromwell I would give my life to be in the picture and he contacted the studio. Warners absolutely refused to lend me out. How could they? They needed me desperately for such historic milestones as *The Big Shakedown* and *The Man With The Black Hat*." (That film was later retitled *Satan Met A Lady*.)

Always a fighter, she wouldn't take no for an answer. So she went to war. "I begged, implored, cajoled. I haunted Jack Warner's office. Every single day I arrived at his door with the shoeshine boy. The part of Mildred was something I had to have. I spent six months in supplication and drove Mr. Warner to the point of desperation, desperate enough to say yes, anything to get rid of me. My employers believed I would hang myself playing such an unpleasant heroine. I had become such a nuisance over the issue I think they identified me with the character and felt we deserved each other."

Shooting began in the spring of 1934. By now she had a very clear picture of Mildred in her mind. She felt that Maugham had painted his character so well that she could use his writing as a textbook for her development of the screen character. Leslie Howard, however, wasn't altogether thrilled with the idea of working with Bette, no matter how enthusiastically she felt about the picture. It was well known that he openly considered her a nobody and believed he personally deserved to be working with a more important actress. But that was only one problem for Bette to overcome. More troublesome was his indifference to her. It seems he refused to go out of his way to cooperate with her. Two actors can work together to make a film better but Howard simply couldn't be bothered. He stood around the set during the first few days of shooting, surrounded by his entourage of British chums and claimed . . . with their agreement . . . that his clipped British accent was absolutely right for his role, while Bette, an American, was all wrong playing a Cockney waitress. Forseeing the accent problem and not wanting to embarrass herself with a weak imitation of a Cockney, Bette went out of her way to prepare for the part. It might be one of the few recorded serious efforts ever made at learning how to speak with King's English in the worst possible manner. Six weeks before shooting began Bette invited a working class Englishwoman into her home and learned to speak a different kind of English. By the time she walked on to the sound stage Bette believed her working class London accent would convince even Howard that she had been 'born within the sound of Bow Bells'.

Howard might well have been impressed although he didn't make any effort to show it. He certainly knew what true Cockney sounded like. The rest of America probably didn't. London was two weeks away by ocean liner and Bette's Cockney, even if it wasn't accurate, would suit most American audiences of 1934 just fine. Today we know better. She changed all her "my's" to "me's" . . . which was O.K. . . . but the rest of the accent comes across these days sounding like a mixture of a southern My Fair Lady and Cary Grant. Oh well, she deserves a lot of points for having tried.

Anyway, John Cromwell was staunchly on her side even if Howard wasn't. Cromwell said, years later, that right from the first day he met Bette he knew she was the actress for the part of Mildred. To start with, he was impressed by her sheer courage. He knew all too well that no other actress in Hollywood would have dared to face the camera the way Bette did as Mildred, with her hair unkempt, in cheap clothes, with a vicious tongue and ugly manner. It wasn't every actress who could successfully pull off a line like, "I'd rather wait for him than have you waiting for me".

Then he said he was impressed by Bette's understanding of Mildred. He said that Bette always gave him the impression that Mildred had been on her feet all day, the way waitresses were in real life. Bette had convinced Cromwell to let her do her own make-up and, while he was prudent to see that she didn't go too far in her disguise, the result on the screen is a girl who looks tired, ill and poor.

Yet Cromwell's most important insight comes when he talks about what he saw going on inside Bette's head. Charles Higham quotes him as saying, "I sensed a desperation in Davis. It wasn't just the desperation of an unhappy woman whose marriage was going wrong. She was frightened, really frightened that the worst thing of all would happen to her as an actress that she would become bored with her work, develop a block and lose her career. Mildred was her chance, once and for all, to make the big time. And yet I never felt she was overdoing it. My faith in her was supported by the knowledge that her greatness would be tempered by discipline."

A description of the plot doesn't really do the story justice. It reads well in book form because Maugham was a masterly writer. A synopsis therefore seems slightly flat. Nevertheless, *Of Human Bondage* is a modern love story played in tragedy. Philip Carey had gone off to Paris as a young man to be a painter. But after four years he realizes he doesn't have what it takes, so he comes home to England and enrols in medical school. His personal failure in Paris and the strength of his desire to help humanity is supposed to pull at the heartstrings. Just in case it misses, Philip is also clubfooted.

Because he is older than the other students and has a physical handicap, you quickly see that he is much more introspective, a more serious and sensitive man who devotes much of his time to his studies. He is almost the exact opposite to Mildred, the waitress with whom he falls in love. But love here does not flower right away because Mildred is involved with a German salesman named Miller. Philip, with his intense feelings, tries to win her. When he finally gets down to proposing marriage, she shrugs him off by announcing that she is going to marry Miller. Heartbroken, Philip throws himself into his studies and settles into a relationship with a woman named Nora. Then Mildred shows up, *sans* Miller but with child. Philip to the rescue. He dumps Nora, sets Mildred up in a flat and all might be well except that Mildred runs off again, this time with Philip's former best friend, Griffiths. Now Philip meets a girl named Sally . . . her father was a patient in the hospital where Philip has been studying and the two fall for each other. Sally tells Philip she loves him for himself and not out of pity for his clubfoot. Philip realizes Sally might be able to help him shed the burden of Mildred . . . except, guess who shows up again! Mildred tells Philip she is sorry she deserted him and begs to be taken back. He agrees. She offers herself to him . . . a sort of payment . . . but ever so righteous, Philip refuses. In a rage, Mildred insults him, then goes about wrecking his apartment, ripping it to shreds. She even destroys the valuable stock securities he needs to sell to continue his education.

No longer able to pay for his schooling, Philip takes a job as a salesman. But now, because he can't bury his sorrow in his studies, he becomes depressed and falls ill. As luck would have it, he is taken into care and nursed back to health. He then discovers that plastic surgery can correct his handicap and informed that he has just inherited enough money to pay for his schooling. As soon as he resumes his studies, he bumps into Griffiths who tells him that Mildred is in the hospital, in a coma . . . then dead. Poor Mildred. But lucky Philip. He turns to Sally and they go off in a taxicab.

Again, laid out on paper like this, the plot seems a bit contrived. Maugham managed, however, to write the story so well that what we might consider corny today was in those days fairly believable. Transposing such an introspective piece of writing on to film is another matter. At one point Nora, referring to Philip's suffering at Mildred's hands, can't understand how he can go back to her. She asks, "After all she has done . . . how could you?" Philip answers, "That's what I'd like to know". He should have said, "That's what the audience would like to know."

True, the film-going public of the '30s was well accustomed to last minute inheritances and chance meetings but this time it was even too much for them. The film previewed to an audience that literally got up and walked out before the final reel. It was too difficult for them to believe that Philip would still be in love with Mildred after all the insults and abuse. Nearly half a century later it's still impossible. In a panic, Pandro Berman ordered the film back to the editing table for some drastic cutting. It didn't help much. Even recut, the film still failed at the box office. Today the reasons seem obvious. Leslie Howard played a much too passive and detached Philip in contrast with Bette's interpretation of Mildred. Bette gave it everything she had.

"I suppose no amount of rationalization can change the fact that we are all made up of good and evil," Bette wrote at one point, showing how well she understood Mildred. Part of her understanding might have come straight out of her personal life at the time. Her marriage was going sour and in some ways Howard might have reminded her of her husband, Ham. You wonder today when you see the film just how Mildred's intense reactions might have been motivated by Bette's annoyance with Howard or Ham. And in her autobiography she openly admits that she never completely became Mildred. Instead, Mildred might have become her. "I was always Bette Davis watching herself become another person. We all, on occasion, find ourselves involved in a character that strikes a painfully personal chord. It is then we must be ruthless with ourselves."

Of course, it should go without saying that whatever her motivations were, what really matters is what comes across on the screen. In this case, it was her first truly superb performance. Even Somerset Maugham praised her work, quite a compliment when you consider that authors almost always complain that a film adaptation never does their writing or characterizations justice. On top of that, the critics who panned the film stopped very short of blaming her. *Of Human Bondage* might not have turned out the way Berman and Cromwell and Howard and Bette hoped but she surpassed all of their expectations and everyone else's too. The *New York Times* gave her top marks for providing "What is easily her finest performance". *Film Weekly* wrote, "A big surprise was the performance given by Bette Davis as the tawdry little waitress. . . . Few people realized that she had the ability to understand and interpret the part so successfully, especially as hitherto she has chiefly been seen as a sex-ridden siren of the *Ex-Lady* type or as the assistant of William Powell and James Cagney in various rackets. Her unsympathetic, but real-life character study, has caused a boom in the Bette Davis stock." And as icing on the cake, *Life Magazine* went as far as to say that Bette Davis in *Of Human Bondage* offered "Probably the best performance ever recorded on the screen by a US actress".

Bette had gambled and all the indications were that she had won. She told an interviewer once the film was out, "I feel I went the limit. The fact that the picture achieved such fine results in no way minimizes my own perception of the risks I was running." Many years after that interview she added that Mildred "was the first leading-lady villainess ever played on a screen for real. I was the female Marlon Brando of my generation."

The impact of Mildred runs deep. She was a thoroughly unattractive character. Anybody who sits through a showing of that film with any sympathy for Mildred has to have gotten it all wrong. You may not weep for Philip but there is no way you can shed a tear for Mildred. Yet the results of playing that role were so positive for Bette that she must have known immediately she had hit on something important. These days it's easy to make the obvious comparison between Mildred and say, Baby Jane. There is, of course, a difference but it lies in the maturity of the bitchiness. And maybe that means Baby Jane could never have happened without Mildred coming along first. It might be fair to say that no other actress in Hollywood in 1962 could have made Baby Jane as evil as she was. No other actress in Hollywood in 1934 dared to play Mildred. If you accept the theory that stars tend to be remembered for one or two roles, or a series of films in which the roles they play are similar, then those roles become a sort of theme. If ever there was such a thing as "A Bette Davis role", she found it in Mildred. Since then, she has simply gotten better at it.

Bette as Mildred opposite Leslie Howard as Philip in Of Human Bondage.

Once *Of Human Bondage* was finished, she had to say goodbye to Pandro Berman's RKO and return to the house that Warner built. Needless to say, she came home reluctantly. Not that the Warners could ignore her triumph even if they wanted to but at Warners even the biggest stars were merely considered employees.

Strangely enough, in a real sense, the big winners of Bette's new fame were the Warners because they still owned her. She was bigger-than-ever box office, and all theirs. A couple of years before she did *Of Human Bondage* she had good reason to believe that she and Jack Warner had very different views as to just who Bette Davis was. She said then that the Warners saw her in those days as an upstart whom they had taken from obscurity and turned into a star. At the same time she saw herself as a serious student of the dramatic possibilities the screen offered and given the opportunity she could achieve great things. Coming back to Warners after *Of Human Bondage* it seems the two still didn't see eye to eye. She was more convinced than ever that she was capable of great screen performances. But she also understood that she would have to have help. She would have to have a great script, a great director and a great supporting cast. It's the natural thing for an actress riding on a success to believe but again, as far as the Warners were concerned, she was merely an employee. Right away they cast her into a film called *Housewife*.

George Brent played Bill, a copywriter who opens his own advertising agency. He's just about to fail when he gets a last minute shot at a big account and lands it. His former sweetheart Patricia, played by Bette, is a copywriter who comes to work for him and tries to rekindle the flame. Bill's wife is less than thrilled about this and tries to get him to fire Patricia. Friction creates flames and Bill's marriage nearly burns up. He goes to court to get a divorce but comes to his senses just in the nick of time, apologizes to his wife and that's the end of Patricia. Love triumphs. The vamp fades away. America is saved by true love. Warners paid their rent.

However, the critics yawned. *They* were *not* employees of the Warners and they could do whatever they wanted. What they wanted to do, and what they put in print, was that *Housewife* was not worthy of Bette's talents. It was directed by Alfred Green who had worked with her in a total of seven films, more than any other single director. In *The Rich Are Always With Us* and *The Dark Horse*, Green tried comedy and missed the mark. In *Parachute Jumper* he managed to create a film that offered Robert Aldrich a lot of material to show just how bad an actress Baby Jane was. *Housewife* was effort number four for Bette and Green and *The Girl From Tenth Avenue* was number five. That film wasn't much either, but if it worked at all it was thanks to Bette. Then came *Dangerous* with Franchot Tone and this time Green managed to bring out Bette's power. It's a classic '30s drama, and one which won her an Academy Award for Best Actress. It's also a point of controversy in her career because there has always been some doubt as to whether she actually earned it with *Dangerous* or was simply given the award late for *Of Human Bondage*. In any case, Green and Bette scored with *Dangerous* and it's almost too bad that they didn't quit while they were ahead. They made another film, *The Golden Arrow* with George Brent. It was meant to be a throwback to *The Rich Are Always With Us,* except that it wasn't funny and no matter how hard Green tried, he couldn't turn Bette Davis and George Brent into a Hepburn/Tracy couple.

The film immediately following *Housewife* was *Bordertown* and in its own way it's a significant film. If *Housewife* gave the impression that Bette's success in *Of Human Bondage* might simply have been a fluke, no one could have believed it once they saw her in *Bordertown*. It was a success which confirmed her success. The story was nowhere as strong as Somerset Maugham's, although Paul Muni as Johnny was good and Bette as Marie was better. The picture was released in January 1935 but obviously made in late 1934. Bette says in her autobiography that she made *Bordertown* before *Of Human Bondage*. She might have. It could have been "put in the can" and held up in post-production while she worked at RKO but then other books about Hollywood in those days show her coming back from RKO to do *Housewife* then *Bordertown*. Yet another source suggests she did *Housewife* before *Of Human Bondage* and

Housewife *with George Brent.*

Bordertown immediately afterwards. The sequence used here is based on something of a general concensus of Bette's many biographers, release dates of films and some minor logic. It's only a small point but it's mentioned to clear up any confusion that might otherwise be mistaken for inaccuracy.

Bordertown is a study in jealousy. Johnny works in the fields during the day and studies law at night. He is admitted to the bar, loses a case through ineptitude and is disbarred. Defeated, he leaves town to find work in a border town saloon . . . probably Tijuana. Bette plays the wife of the man who owns the joint and right away falls for Johnny. But he refuses to betray his new boss. The way out of her marriage and hopefully into Johnny's arms is murder. She manages it and her husband's death is pronounced accidental by the police. At the same time, Johnny falls in love with another woman, played by Margaret Lindsay, and Bette's reaction is a fiercely jealous rage. "You're riff-raff and so am I," she screams at Johnny. "You belong to me and you're gonna stay with me because I'm holdin' on to ya. I committed murder to getcha." Johnny tries to free himself of her and she finally confesses to the crime. Except that she implicates Johnny as her accomplice. All looks extremely black for him until Marie takes the stand at the trial and goes into a state of mental collapse. Johnny is cleared and Marie is carted off. He returns to Margaret Lindsay, but now she says she's no longer in love with him. Through his jealousy she falls victim to a fatal accident. As the film ends, Johnny returns to the town where he was born, to work again in the fields where he started.

When the reviewers got hold of this film they almost all agreed that the high point of it was Bette's performance. She played Marie with the same enthusiasm that she played Mildred. The studio advertised the film with posters saying, "The Beautiful Hellcat of *Of Human Bondage* flings a challenge to the dynamic star of *I Am A Fugitive*. Heaven help her when she finds out what a man she's talking to." *Film Weekly* praised her interpretation of "A fiery-souled, half-witted, love-crazed woman" as being "so cleverly done that one finds oneself being convinced in spite of one's better judgement." The *New York Times* wrote, "Miss Davis plays the part with the ugly, sadistic and utterly convincing sense of reality which distinguished her fine performance in *Of Human Bondage*." Whitney Stine, in *Mother Goddam* felt that *Bordertown* made it clear that Bette "Was a new kind of actress playing a new kind of woman. Critics, bored by the goody-two-shoes style of acting so prevalent among Hollywood females of the period, were caught up short by her power."

And power is the right word. In the murder scene she showed a powerful sense of the macabre. In the courtroom scene where she goes off her head, she showed that she could produce moments of sheer horror, not by yelling or screaming but by subtle underplaying and great insights into a mentally ill character. That she was consciously developing the ability to overpower audiences with fear is really a hint of things to come.

It was easy to see that her future as an actress did not lie in films like *Housewife*. Mildred and Marie were her future. In a 1935 article for *Film Weekly* entitled "It Pays To Be Typed" you come across what might be the first indications of the character she was planning to create for herself.

"The most difficult thing to do," she wrote, "either on the screen or on the stage is to go on playing oneself, being oneself and still remain interesting. The easiest thing in the world is to play a character role. At least I have found it so." Eventually she confessed in that article, "Let's face it. It is useless to disguise the fact that to become popular and keep her popularity, a Hollywood actress has to establish a definite screen style, an identity to which one must frankly attach that horrible description, 'type'. Once she has discovered a style which the public acclaims, she must retain more or less the same 'type' in every picture she makes."

At the time she was almost certainly thinking about the type she played in *Cabin In The Cotton*. She very much liked the character of Madge and felt comfortable. What she didn't know at the time was that whilst she had the right idea, she had the wrong role. Playing the Madge types of this world could make her a star. It would, however, be the Mildred types and the Marie types that would make her a legend.

Darryl Zanuck (top) and Michael Curtiz.

Best Actress

"I HAVE A PRETTY healthy temper," she once told an interviewer. "Most of the time I fight it's with film people and that's just self-preservation."

That was the case with the ending of *Bordertown*. She believed she had to play Marie in a certain way especially in the courtroom scene where she goes mad. Archie Mayo and Jack Warner believed she should shriek and pull her hair. In short, they wanted her to be a raving lunatic because that's the way mental breakdowns had always been portrayed. She put up a huge fight and underplayed the scene just enough. The film was put into the can and Warner called Bette into his office. He argued that no one would know Marie was insane by the way Bette played the scene. She snapped back that if, once the film was previewed, that should prove to be the case, she'd re-do the scene. "I was never asked to do a retake," Bette wrote in *Mother Goddam*, eventually adding, "I wanted to be known as an actress, not necessarily a star."

She won her point but it didn't help win her a lot of friends. And before too long she'd be needing friends.

While all this was going on, Frank Capra, then one of Columbia's bright young directors, was looking for the female lead of *It Happened One Night*. Bette's name came up but Jack Warner wouldn't loan her out. He too had a few points to prove. The part went to Claudette Colbert. So did the Academy Award for Best Actress and Bette's chance to work with Clark Gable.

Then the Warners came up with a picture for her called *The Case Of The Howling Dog*. Bette refused to do it. Warner suspended her and notified the rest of the town that she wasn't available for any pictures anywhere until she settled her differences with Warners. It seems a number of other directors in Hollywood were interested in working with her including Mervyn Leroy at RKO for the lead in *Sweet Adeline,* a Jerome Kern musical. Bette's name had also been suggested for the lead in a Damon Runyon story *Hold 'Em Yale* where she would have played opposite George Raft. But no, said Warner, she wasn't going to work anywhere until she came back to the fold.

Then came the Academy Awards. It looked as if Bette were a certainty for her portrayal of Mildred. But looks can be deceiving. The award went to Colbert and a minor scandal followed. Ever since that year an independent firm of accountants has been called in to count the ballots for those awards. Bette lost the Oscar, but she had unknowingly won a few big battles along the way. The cry of foul when she turned up a loser changed the system forever and the publicity she got while that scandal raged did her career an enormous amount of good.

Unfortunately Jack and his brothers just couldn't see Bette for the actress she was. "There was no change in the Warner attitude after all this acclaim," she said in *The Lonely Life*. "I was made to trudge through the professional swamp at Warners brimming over with frustration and rage. One skirmish after another followed *Bondage*."

Bette was out of work for two weeks before she and the Warners temporarily shelved their differences. "The Warners were quite befuddled by me at this point," she went on in her autobiography. "No matter what piece of garbage they gave me to do and no matter how much I scornfully sniffed at it, I did my job, and well."

Her attitude was that if they wouldn't help her, she'd help herself. The critics and the public could see how good she was so she was winning on that side. But then all she had to do was look around the studio to see what else was being made to know that there were

Bette Davis and Shirley Temple at the Academy Award ceremony in 1935.

indeed stories which fitted her.

The three she made right after *Bordertown*, certainly were not among them.

The first was *The Girl From Tenth Avenue*, called *Men On Her Mind* in England. She played Miriam to Ian Hunter's Geoffrey. Miriam is a New York working girl who stumbles across a drunk lawyer and has the kindness to bring him home to sober up. It seems his girl friend has just married someone else. He appreciates Miriam's kindness and, if you can believe this, they decide to get married. Then the ex-girl friend's marriage goes bad and she wants Geoffrey back. In the end Miriam wins but the film is a loser. "The performance she (Bette) gives," wrote Variety, "should pull the picture through". The *New York Times* reviewer called the film, "Modestly stimulating instead of just old potatoes," but described Bette as, "One of the most competent of our younger screen actresses."

Next on the list was *Front Page Woman*, based on a story with the slightly ludicrous title *Women Are Bum Newspapermen*. Michael Curtiz directed. George Brent plays Curt Devlin, ace reporter for *The Daily Express* who happens to be in love with Bette's Ellen Garfield, ace reporter for *The Daily Star*. Needless to say, she comes up with a big story which he says is just a stroke of luck. When she can't follow through, he does. She gets fired, he looks like he'll win the Pulitzer, except that she won't quit and comes through with a written confession from the murderer and Curt Devlin, who once said that women are bum newspapermen, must now take it back.

The real newspapermen decided the film was "a bit on the whimsey side'. They only called it "satisfying entertainment" and gave the cast credit for "a neat sense of comedy".

The third of what Bette has described as 'three stinkers" was *Special Agent*, yet another George Brent epic. Ricardo Cortez plays Nick Carston, famous gangster and Brent plays Bill Bradford, famous part-time newspaperman and full-time undercover agent. Bette's role is Julie Gardner, famous bookkeeper for Carston's mob. Bill befriends Julie so that Julie betrays Nick so that Nick's guys can abduct Julie so that Bill can come to the rescue. "It has all been done before," wrote the *New York Times*, "but somehow it never seems to lose it's visual excitement." The best the *Motion Picture Herald* could think of was the moral "Crime doesn't pay."

In spite of Bette's willingness to fight for what she believed in, with three films like that to her record, it looked as though there might be no escape for her. It looked as though the Warners were still unwilling to back her at the box office with a great script. But just in the nick of time . . . as such things seem to happen in Hollywood . . . along came a property called *Hard Luck Dame*.

Supposedly based on the true life story of actress Jeanne Eagels, Bette played Joyce Heath, a former stage actress who has become a drunk because she feels she is a jinx to everybody and everything. An architect named Dan Bellows finds her . . . that role went to Franchot Tone . . . and he manages through great sacrifice to put her life back together. Joyce naturally falls for Dan but she's already married to Gordon who won't give her a divorce. When he refuses she tries to kill him. It doesn't work. Dan puts her back on the stage, making her a star again and she then returns to Gordon hoping she can put her life with him back together again too.

With the usual Warners supporting cast . . . people like Margaret Lindsay, Alison Skipworth, John Eldredge, Dick Foran, et al. . . . plus the adequate direction of Alfred Green, the fine camera work of Ernest Haller, the make-up of Perc Westmore and the costumes of Orry-Kelly, Bette found herself riding a winner.

The film's title was changed to *Dangerous* and if you can get through some of the soap-opera dialogue, it's a wonderful showcase for Bette's talents. Charles Higham, in *Bette* felt, "This tissue of nonsense would have sunk most actresses at the start but Bette gave the role of the actress an extraordinary realism." In many ways, he was simply echoing the praise of the critics forty-six years before. The reviewer for *The Picture Post* must have been totally haunted by Bette because he wrote, "Bette Davis would probably have been burned as a witch if she had lived two or three hundred years ago. She gives a curious feeling of being charged with power which can find no ordinary outlet. Although the *New York Times'* review was mixed there was note-worthy praise. "That Bette Davis has been unable to match the grim standard she set as Mildred in *Of Human Bondage* is not to her discredit," they said, "In *Dangerous* . . . she tries again. Exept for a few sequences where the tension is convincing as well as deadly, she fails." Yet they did add, "This Davis girl is rapidly becoming one of the most interesting of our screen actresses." And as for that point, the *Los Angeles Times* couldn't have agreed more. "Bette Davis seems actual flesh and blood in *Dangerous*. That's how penetratingly alive she is and how electric, varied as to mood and real her performance in the picture."

Proving that she was more interested in acting than in being a glamour girl, Bette works her first scene without make-up, with her hair uncombed, wearing a very unflattering pair of men's pyjamas and a bathrobe. Haller even photographed her during that first scene with rather stark lighting. The effect is one that works well to show a woman who is truly down and out.

Again, if you can get past some of the appalling dialogue and the wooden perform-ance by Franchot Tone, the film is still worth seeing. Of course, the obvious comparison then as now is between the characters of Joyce in *Dangerous* and Mildred in *Of Human Bondage*. Almost all the reviewers suggested it, but Bette thought in *Mother Goddam* that the comparison was unfair and that there were too many differences in both the stories and characterizations.

As one critic said about her during this period, "Perhaps more than any other modern actress, Bette Davis has been an experimenter. She has often gambled with her popularity. She has always had great courage, in attempting difficult and dangerous parts, unsympathetic characters, roles which no other leading female star would ever contemplate playing."

Next came *The Petrified Forest*. Because the Bette Davis/Leslie Howard team had scored once, Warners probably figured it would work again. Bette was cast as Gabrielle, a waitress who wants to study art in France but is stuck somewhere in the middle of the Arizona desert, working in her father's truck-stop hash house. Howard, British accent and all, literally walks into her life. Based on a play by Robert Sherwood, Howard and Humphrey Bogart had both been in the stage version earlier that year. And it was Howard, once he was cast for the film, who insisted that Bogart be brought along to recreate his role of tough guy criminal Duke Mantee. Bogart had played the part for nearly 200 performances on stage, and by this time could talk out of the side of his mouth with very little effort.

Howard, as Alan Squier, falls for Gabrielle . . . who calls herself Gaby . . . and the two of them eventually make plans to go to France. But Mantee and his gang are on the run and they take over the gas station/cafe as the site of the final shoot-out. When all looks blackest, Squier signs his insurance policy over to Gaby then asks that Mantee shoot him thus giving her the money she needs to get to France. The film stands as a good example of Bette's ability to play a certain type of role. Where she could be harsh as the waitress Mildred, she could also be fragile and vulnerable as the waitress Gaby. To make sure that no one could mistake her for Joyce Heath, she and make-up artist Perc Westmore let her hair go back to it's natural "ash blonde" colour. Rumour has it that Hal Wallis didn't notice for a year and a half!

Produced by Henry Blanke, *The Petrified Forest* was directed by Archie Mayo, the same man who directed her in *Bordertown*. The similarities in the two films are obvious enough but this time the script is meatier and Duke Mantee is so tough that you can't help but wonder what the film would have turned out to be had it been directed by someone like Michael Curtiz. It might even have been an easier film for Bette because, as it was, this one was filled with problems.

By the end of *Dangerous* she was certain that she had enough power to make her feelings known and get results but it didn't quite turn out that way. She wanted to go to RKO to play Queen Elizabeth opposite Katharine Hepburn who had the title role in *Mary of Scotland*. Warner said no. Then she wanted to go to Parmount to play the lead in their production of *Alice in Wonderland* with Gary Cooper as The White

Knight. Warner said no again but offered her Gaby in *The Petrified Forest*. It was, he pointed out, the pivotal role in the film although it was not the lead. He also promised her billing above the title. The play had been a big enough stage hit that the film was an attractive proposition but she had reservations about working with Leslie Howard. After all, she well remembered that Howard wasn't exactly overjoyed about working with her in *Of Human Bondage* and she feared the two of them would go through the same thing again. Jack Warner assured Bette however that Howard's opinions had changed. If they had Bette didn't see it on the set. He remained himself and didn't seem to care much about being pleasant or cordial to her. Then there was Bogart. She was never too crazy about him, had never been his biggest fan and as far as she was concerned, he still annoyed her. Then there was the sand. Everytime they shot exteriors, Mayo turned on the fans and blew the stuff right into his actors' faces. She started to get ill. Howard didn't get along with Mayo and repeatedly delayed production whenever, and however, he could. As the shooting continued Bette caught a cold which affected her voice and annoyed Mayo. At one point she badly sprained her ankle on the set and shooting schedules had to be rearranged to work around her. Then in one scene, Mayo turned on the fans to blow the sand and Bette got so sick that there was some concern she might not be able to finish the picture.

The end result was that Duke Mantee made Humphrey Bogart a star. The film didn't hurt Bette's reputation but it did much more for Bogart's. The critics liked Leslie Howard sufficiently to ignore the incongruity of his British accent in the middle of the Southwest. Archie Mayo's direction was referred to cryptically as "canny but respectful" and Bette's reviews were fine. The *New York Times* said, "There should be a large measure of praise for Bette Davis who demonstrates that she does not have to be hysterical to be credited with a grand performance."

Then real trouble started to brew. Warner sent Bette her next script. It was based on Dashiell Hammett's *The Maltese Falcon* but was called *The Man With The Black Hat*. At first sight, Bette hated it. At second glance, she hated it even more. Instead of a third look, she simply refused to do it. Warner insisted. She referred him to her attorneys. Warner's attorneys went to see her. She still refused to do the film. Warner refused to let her off. Bette was having problems at home and couldn't afford to get fired. A compromise was worked out. She finally agreed to do the film when Warner agreed to let her do a guest appearance on Al Jolson's radio programme where she played a scene from *Dangerous*. She upheld her part of the deal and suffered her way through *The Man With The Black Hat* which was later called *Satan Met A Lady*.

Directed by William Dieterle, this was the second time the story had been filmed. It was also the worst. Ricardo Cortez and Bebe Daniels did it first in 1931. Bogart and Mary Astor did it best in 1941. In this version, the script-writers changed the falcon to a jewelled ram's horn. Warren William played the detective but instead of peppering the film with characters like Caspar Gutman, played in 1941 by Sydney Greenstreet, this time that part went to Alison Skipworth. You figure it out. Bosley Crowther at the *New York Times* couldn't. "After viewing *Satan Met A Lady*" he wrote, "all thinking people must acknowledge that a Bette Davis Reclamation Project to prevent the waste of this gifted lady's talents would not be a too-drastic addition to our various programmes for the conservation of natural resources." That was the kindest thing he had to say about the film. Most of the time he felt, "So disconnected and lunatic are the picture's ingredients, so irrelevant and monstrous its people, that one lives through it in a constant expectation of seeing a group of uniformed individuals appear suddenly from behind the furniture and take the entire cast into protective custody. There is no story, merely a farrago of nonsense representing a series of practical studio compromises with an unworkable script."

Warner added insult to injury by immediately calling upon Bette to work in another loser called *The Golden Arrow*. It was a film version of a Michael Arlan play directed by Alfred E. Green which Kay Francis had already refused and Warner had let her off. Bette had wanted to play the lead in *Anthony Adverse* but Warner had given that part to Olivia de Havilland. They wanted Bette for *The Golden Arrow* opposite George

Brent. She plays Daisy, a girl who works in a cafeteria but poses as an heiress. Brent plays Johnny, an ace reporter who is someday going to be a famous novelist. Of course at the end the two get married. In between, they get a lot of black eyes. The whole thing is worth missing.

Bette thought so too because during the shooting she walked off the set. She claimed ill health and exhaustion. Later she admitted, "I was actually insulted to have to appear in such a cheap, nothing story as *The Golden Arrow*. . . ."

Then the list of nominations for the Academy Awards was announced and she was suddenly a candidate for Best Actress. It got her moving on the picture again. *The Golden Arrow* was released before *Satan Met A Lady*, in spite of the fact that it was made afterwards. But before either of them went out to the public, Bette won her first Academy Award. She was named Best Actress for her part in *Dangerous*, besting Katharine Hepburn, Merle Oberon, Claudette Colbert, Elisabeth Bergner and Miriam Hopkins. In *The Lonely Life* however, she called the award "A consolation prize," and admitted, "This nagged at me. It was true that even if the honor had been earned, it had been earned last year. There was no doubt that Hepburn's performance deserved the award." And years later she continued to believe that, by saying, "It's common knowledge that I got this first Oscar as a sort of delayed reward for *Of Human Bondage*."

Whatever the reason, she had it and the Brothers Warner knew it. They even, much to her horror, advertised the Best Actress award when they released *The Golden Arrow*. That might have helped sell seats in the movie house but the award had another effect. For the first time since she got to Hollywood Bette realized that she truly was a star. There was something of a sense of security in knowing that she owned the award and owning it meant, at least for a while, that she could work anywhere.

She started demanding her rights. She wanted vacation time, she wanted more money, she wanted to do a picture a year outside Warners and she wanted to be treated like a star. Jack Warner fought back, saying that the old contract was still valid and there was no reason to negotiate a new one. Then he offered her a role in *God's Country and The Woman* where she would play a lumberjack. Bette was incredulous. She absolutely and totally refused, willing in fact to risk her entire career and never work again. Warner tried bargaining. He said he had just bought an option on a novel and if she would do as she was told he'd cast her as the star. The novel was called *Gone With The Wind*. Her famous reply to him was, "I bet it's a pip."

The fight with Warner went on through the spring. The studio bosses were now offering her $2000 a week with increases over the next five years. But this was not simply a question of money as far as Bette was concerned. She wanted better scripts and she was willing to risk her entire career to get them. She had fought the system this far and she was willing to go all the way. There was a big meeting in Warner's office in the middle of June which ended rather abruptly when Bette walked out. She turned Warner down flat. In return, Warner turned her down. The studio legal office sent her a note saying that if she did not report on time for *God's Country And The Woman*, she would be suspended and sued for damages.

The fight with Warners made headlines. And while Bette nervously stood her ground, those headlines reached England. A producer named Toeplatz saw them and thought he might have a chance at making films with her. He offered Bette $50,000 for her services in two films. The first was to be *I'll Take The Low Road* with Douglass Montgomery and Nigel Bruce. The second, seemingly without a working title, was to star Maurice Chevalier. Bette must have understood that her contract with Warners prevented such a move and Toeplatz must have known it as well. But he made his offer and Bette jumped at the chance.

She went to England, only to be met on her arrival with a court order preventing her from working there. She decided to take her case to court. On October 20, 1936 the Associated Press reported in most American newspapers that Bette had lost. "Bette Davis, American film player, was restrained yesterday from appearing in motion pictures or other performances in England for any company except Warner Brothers of Hollywood." The AP story said that Bette's attorneys had based their case on the contention that her contract with Warners was so stringent that it constituted "restraint of trade".

The British Courts didn't agree. Bette decided to appeal. Then George Arliss reappeared in her life. With a voice she trusted, he suggested she swallow a little of her pride and go back to Hollywood. "Go back gracefully and accept the decision," he supposedly counselled her. "You haven't lost as much as you think."

Warner himself had gone to England to testify and the moment the decision went in his favour he played it for all it was worth. He knew the power of good publicity so he told the press just how generous he was going to be about the matter. He announced that all was forgiven and Bette could come home. He promised to pick up half her legal expenses, drop his damages claim against her, raise her salary and give her a decent script. But Warner had an ulterior motive. Had Bette somehow won in England and the British courts overthrown her contract letting her become what is these days in sport is called a "free agent", the studio system would have died a very sudden death. Every contract player in Hollywood would have walked off the lots and no studio could afford that. As it was, Bette's case did seem to lend moral support to a few others with legal problems, among them Olivia de Havilland who eventually fought the idea that a studio could suspend an actor. Her case came up in California and she won, making a big change in the system to the benefit of every actor in town.

So Bette returned to Hollywood and even if she was a loser in London, she had, as Arliss promised, not lost as much as she imagined in Los Angeles. "It was now evident to them," she said in *The Lonely Life,* referring to the Warners, "that I never would have sacrificed so much time, energy and money unless I was indeed earnest about my career." She said she knew she had to make the best of the situation, so she met the Warners in the spirit of conciliation. "In a way, my defeat was a victory. At last we were seeing eye to eye on my career. I was aching to work and they were eager to encourage me."

The story Warner offered her was based on the real-life character, Lucky Luciano. The film was called *Marked Woman.* Bette played Mary, a dance-hall girl who works for, and lies to protect, the gangster Johnny Vanning. That part was well played by Eduardo Ciannelli. But when one of Vanning's friends kills Mary's sister she decides to go after him and get revenge by sending him to jail. She turns against him with the help of the assistant district attorney, David Graham, played by Humphrey Bogart. Justice triumphs over evil but not before a lot of people get beaten up and Mary is nearly killed. One of Vanning's henchmen is played by Ben Weldon. Had luck been on his side, he might have somehow emerged as one of Hollywood's all-time great heavies. He not only acts the part, portraying a cold-blooded thug, he also looks like one.

Bogart didn't make his appearance until somewhere around the middle of the second reel and this time, instead of being Duke Mantee, he shows a lot more polish. He's a lot more believable playing the young lawyer than he was the year before playing Duke. He probably became a star the day he took that polish and used it to patina his really tough guy roles. As for Bette, she's at her best when she's yelling at someone, either Bogart or Jane Bryan who played her ill-fated sister.

One of the nice stories that emerged from this film had to do with Bette's bandages when she's lying in a hospital bed and Bogart comes to see her, trying to convince her to talk. The studio make-up people bandaged her for the scene, but she didn't like it. When they broke for lunch, she went to her own doctor, told him what she wanted, and he bandaged her the way he would a woman who had just been beaten up and scarred. When she drove back onto the lot, the guard at the gate took one look at her and rang the set to announce that Miss Davis had been in a serious car accident. The director Lloyd Bacon rushed to her when he found her to ask what had happened, obviously fearing that his film would now be delayed. She explained that she was only getting her make-up to look correct. He objected but she struck back with something like, "You believed it was real. The audiences will too!"

In Bordertown *with Paul Muni.*

With Franchot Tone in Dangerous, *for which she won her first Academy Award as Best Actress.*

When the picture was released, the reviews confirmed her earlier enthusiasm for the script. The *New York Sun* felt, "*Marked Woman* gives Bette Davis the type of role she handles so well." Variety wrote, "There is little doubt that as an actress Bette Davis has got it and *Marked Woman* will help cement that fact." And the *New York Times* added, "Apparently the Warners meant it when they invited the runaway Bette Davis to 'come home; all is forgiven.' In *Marked Woman*, which celebrates the prodigal's return, they have offered up, fortunately not for sacrifice, a dramatically concise script, a shrewd director and an extremely capable supporting cast. Not to be outdone, Miss Davis has turned in her best performance since she cut Leslie Howard to the quick in *Of Human Bondage*."

Thirty years or so later, one of America's most astute film critics, Pauline Kael, wrote that Bette Davis in this film was "the embodiment of the sensational side of the '30s movies." But then it seems that somewhere towards the mid '60s the CBS television network cancelled a scheduled showing of the film because the central characters play prostitutes, even if they are disguised as dance-hall girls, and, said CBS "This type of thing shouldn't be fed into the home."

This type of thing went down well with the movie going public of 1937 and for years Jack Warner said it was his favourite Bette Davis picture. He must have been pleased because the film he gave her to follow *Marked Woman* stands as one of the all-time great boxing epics. Directed by Michael Curtiz and starring Edward G. Robinson, it is very much a classic of the era. But had Warner kept a now forgotten promise, things might have been a little different for Bette. Before she left for England he had spoken to her about buying the rights to *Gone With The Wind*. In the end, it was his rival David O. Selznick who picked up the rights. Realizing the potential of the film, and never being one to let a good business deal slip through his hands, Warner went to Selznick and offered to be the film's distributor. Selznick may have been interested but Warner had some conditions. Errol Flynn had to be Rhett Butler and Bette Davis had to be Scarlett O'Hara. Selznick obviously put out some feelers only to find that Bette wouldn't be so anxious to play with Flynn. By the time Selznick had gotten around to Clark Gable he had also gotten around to Vivien Leigh. Bette feels she missed her chance to play the best female role in the history of the movies. If nothing else, she certainly missed out on yet again making film history. "It could have been written for me," she said about the script of *Gone With The Wind*. "When I read it and remembered Mr. Warner's promise, I was fit to be tied." In *Bette*, Charles Higham actually wonders whether or not Bette would have made a good Scarlett. It's an interesting point. Bette's previous biographers probably would have agreed with Bette herself in thinking she would have been fantastic. Higham, on the other hand, is a little more realistic about his evaluation. He feels that while Bette might have brought more thought and feeling to the role, "her lack of sheer beauty might have told against her in the long run." He reasons that Scarlett was a perennial tease and a prize worth pursuing and that for all her talent and even for all her good looks, "Bette Davis could never have answered that description."

So instead she made *Kid Galahad*, playing Fluff Phillips, a barroom singer and girl friend of Nick the fight promoter, played by Edward G. The boxer Galahad is played by Wayne Morris, and he becomes the champ but it costs Nick his life in a shoot-out with Turkey Morgan, portrayed by Humphrey Bogart. The fight scenes are well staged, Edward G. does one of his great dying scenes and Bette was no longer the object of Curtiz's scorn. It was a man's picture, very much a film for Edward G. but one in which Bette managed to prove herself to an audience who didn't necessarily know her the way the women of America did. And it was the women of America who got to see her next in *That Certain Woman*. A remake of an earlier Gloria Swanson hit, the storyline has often been described as "unmitigated suds." Bette as Mary is a young widow thanks to the St. Valentine's Day massacre. Working for a lawyer, she meets Jack, played by Henry Fonda, who falls in love with her. The two elope but Jack's father sees to it that the marriage is annulled. What follows is right out of afternoon television. She bears a son. Jack remarries. The lawyer dies leaving some of his money

Petrified Forest *with Leslie Howard and Humphrey Bogart, whose career the film launched.*

Kid Galahad *with Edward G.*

to Mary. The lawyer's widow suspects the child is really her late husband's. Jack rescues Mary by swearing it's his. She goes off to Europe on the lawyer's money. When Jack's wife dies he comes to her and again swears his love.

The critics said she showed "commendable versatility" and performed "valiantly," and if nothing else she got a chance to kiss Henry Fonda. The story goes that they met for the first time when she was sixteen and Fonda was seventeen. One evening, in Princeton, New Jersey, they found themselves in the back seat of a car and Fonda shyly pecked her on the cheek. As Fonda told *Playboy*, that night was "a hundred years ago" and in those days he didn't find Bette very attractive. Anyway, he was shy with girls. "I just leaned over and gave her a peck . . . that's all it was." A few days later he said he got a letter from Bette informing him that she had told her mother about the kiss and that Ruthie would soon announce their engagement. Fonda said to *Playboy*, "Never answered it. Never paid any more attention. Never heard anything more." According to Bette, the two of them met a few years later, and worked together for a week in a play at the theatre on Cape Cod. He was passing through and she was in love with him. But it still seemed to be one-sided. For *That Certain Woman*, their kisses are recorded on film. The next time they kissed, it was for *Jezebel*, and this time those kisses helped get her Oscar No. 2.

Between kisses came yet another picture, her fourth in 1937. *It's Love I'm After* was another Archie Mayo directed event with Bette and Leslie Howard, Olivia de Havilland and a smattering of such Warner regulars as Patric Knowles, Grace Fields and Spring Byington. Bette and Leslie Howard play a stage couple not unlike Alfred Lunt and Lynn Fontanne except they fight a lot in private. They have set a date to be married no less than eleven times but never quite get it together to tie the knot. You know how the film ends. Bette didn't much like the film but the reviewers laughed, calling it a "diverting comedy."

While doing *It's Love I'm After*, she put in a bid for a small role in a Paul Muni film called *The Life Of Emile Zola*. But big stars didn't do small roles in those days and everybody who had anything to say about it said no, including Muni. She might have let that slip by except that she found herself in another battle with the studio. They had her slotted for a film called *Hollywood Hotel*. Thoroughly exhausted, she had herself slotted for a vacation at the beach. It was summer and she wanted a rest. Hal Wallis said no and ordered her to a costume fitting. Bette didn't show up. It looked as if the truce was over and the Brothers Warner were now going back to their old attitude. Only when she suffered second-degree burns on the beach and contracted a fever was she taken off the film and given her rest.

Then came *Jezebel*. It wasn't Scarlett O'Hara but it certainly was close.

Miriam Hopkins had starred in it on Broadway but the play closed quickly. Some years later, as part of a settlement in a contractual disagreement completely independent of Bette, Jack Warner bought the film rights to *Jezebel*. She had personally championed the cause and when Warner asked her who'd want to see a film about a girl who wears a red dress to a ball, Bette answered, "Ten million women." That was good enough for Warner. Making it even better was the fact that Selznick's *Gone With The Wind* would not be out for quite a while and here was a fairly similar story. At least, it was a love story set in the deep south. And while he steadfastly denied Selznick's later accusations that he made *Jezebel* deliberately to sabotage *Gone With The Wind*, looking back, it doesn't look as if Mr. Warner was entirely honest.

Everything for *Jezebel* seemed set. William Wyler was to direct, John Huston had contributed to the screenplay, Ernest Haller was on camera and Orry-Kelly was designing the clothes. Her co-stars were Henry Fonda, George Brent, Donald Crisp, Fay Bainter, Margaret Lindsay and the rest of the usual Warner players. The budget was set at $1.25 million, a staggering sum of money in those days.

Bette played Julie, the beautiful but thoroughly spoiled belle of New Orleans, with two men in love with her – Fonda as Pres and Brent as Buck. In a juvenile attempt to get even with Pres and make some sort of sensational appearance at the Mardi Gras Comos Ball Julie does not conform to the usual white dress like the rest of the ladies but wears a dark red gown. She shocks the town. Pres breaks off his engagement with her and goes north on business. Julie retreats into semi-seclusion for three years until she learns that Pres is coming back. Thinking they will now be married, she plans a large party for him. When he arrives he has a wife in tow. There is a question of honour at stake and Pres' brother duels with Buck and kills him. Then there is an outbreak of yellowjack fever. Among the victims is Pres who must be moved out of town in order to recover. Naturally his wife, played by Margaret Lindsay, wants to be at his side but Julie manages to talk her out of it saying that only a southern woman would know how to best care for him. "Amy, of course it's your right to go. You're his wife. But are you fit to go? Lovin' him isn't enough. If you gave him all your strength, would it be enough? Do you know the Creole word for fever powder? For food and water? His life and yours will hang on just things like that." Huston's talent as a scriptwriter was clearly evident and Wyler's talent as a director even more so. He had throughout his career not only understood the film medium but was also blessed with a deep understanding of drama. Bette makes that point in *The Lonely Life* when she describes her opening scene in the film.

Julie arrives home late for a party wearing a riding habit. As she enters the house, she lifts her skirt with a riding crop. Bette wrote that while it sounds simple, Wyler asked her to take the skirt and crop home to rehearse with them. "The next morning I arrived knowing he was after something special. I made my entrance a dozen times and he wasn't satisfied. He wanted something, all right. He wanted a complete establishment of character with one gesture." She went through forty-five takes to get it.

The most famous scene in the film is, of course, the ball. Wyler shot it without a word of dialogue which was an extremely brave thing to do.

There were, however, a few problems during the production. Fonda had to rush through some of his scenes so that he could get back east for the birth of his daughter, Jane. Because he was a perfectionist, Wyler quickly fell behind schedule. When he was nearly one month late, on a film that was scheduled for about five months of shooting, Warner stepped in. With so much money at stake, he threatened to fire Wyler. Now Bette made a stand. Years before, Wyler had been the director on a test she did and had made some sort of snide comment about actresses who show off their chests to get parts. When she heard he was directing *Jezebel* she went to his office and confronted him with the remark. He told her he honestly didn't remember the incident and that anyway, he was a much nicer person now. Whatever anger she felt went straight out the window. So when he needed her, she showed just how much she respected him by championing his cause with Jack Warner. She said she'd work overtime to keep Wyler on the film and that if Warner pulled him off, it would be a disaster. She made her point and Wyler was permitted to finish the picture.

J.421

Stardom

"*JEZEBEL* REMAINS ONE of her most stirring and beautiful vehicles," wrote Gary Arnold in the *Washington Post* but Bette gave most of the credit to Wyler. She told him, "Anyone who doubts Wyler's genius only has to look at the ballroom sequence. What a wonderful sequence that is. And do you know what we began with? Virtually nothing. It began with a single line in the script: 'Julie goes to the ball.' Wyler was responsible for all the elaboration you see on the screen."

She said in that interview that she desperately wanted Warner to make the film in colour but in those days the studio made only two colour pictures per year. "I would beg and plead and never get it because they knew I was safe money without it. They rejected it as an unnecessary expense."

Arnold also raises the loss of Scarlett's role in *Gone With The Wind* but Bette now sees *Jezebel* as near compensation. "After *Jezebel* I couldn't feel as bad about losing out on Scarlett. The same energies went into the role of Julie and I derived great satisfaction from it." Anyway, she says, not playing Scarlett was her own fault. "I was too mad at Jack Warner to listen to anything he said. When he begged me not to walk out because he'd optioned some Southern novel with a marvellous role for me, I wasn't impressed."

As it was, *Jezebel* and Bette did each other proud. An enormous wave of publicity followed the film and the critics who saw it generally raved. The public responded in kind, agreeing with reviewers who said, "At the centre of it is Bette Davis, growing into an artistic maturity that is one of the wonders of Hollywood. The erratic and tempestuous career of this actress has saved her from playing sweet heroines and glamour girls and given her chances at parts that most players out for popularity would balk at. The result is an experience that has made her unique, in a field of character creation that is practically empty. Her Julie is the peak of her accomplishments, so far, and what is ahead is unpredictable, depending on her luck and the wisdom of her producers."

What turned out to be ahead was her second Academy Award for Best Actress. But that was a year away and in the meantime she was having problems with her personal life. The pressures upon her, perhaps because of those problems, resulted in more friction at the studio. She wanted a new contract, fought for it and got one although it was not exactly what she had hoped for. Warner and Wallis sent her a script called *Comet Over Broadway* which she immediately turned down, so they then sent her a script called *Garden Of The Moon* which she also turned down. It seems she got herself suspended again and the full page ad. for *Jezebel* that ran in *Motion Picture Daily* was face to face with a story headlined "Bette Davis Suspended". When she and Warner managed to come to terms again it was for a film called *The Sisters*. Bette, by the way, was not the only person at Warners turning down roles. She played Louise in this film but finding someone to play her leading man, Frank, was not so easy. First Fredric March said no. Then Franchot Tone said no. Then George Brent said no. It had nothing to do with Bette, it was just that the script didn't interest them. Jack Warner finally talked Errol Flynn into it at his reported $4500 a week salary, almost twice what Bette was making at this time. But the way she saw it, she was there to work and he was there to chase girls. "Flanked by four to six blondes, arms linked, Errol would strut in at about eleven," she wrote, making a point of saying that Flynn was totally indifferent to the acting profession. Whilst he had great charm, his interests were not the same as Bette's. She says in *Mother Goddam* that she was delighted with the part because it was a change of pace. His name on the film would assure a certain audience. But

In Jezebel.

when Warners didn't plan on putting her name above the title with his she fought until they gave in.

The Sisters was directed by Anatole Litvak who was already considered a major European director when he came to the States in the mid-'30s to escape Nazi Germany. He married Miriam Hopkins, who some books have it had been brought onto the Warner lot as a Bette Davis substitute, just in case the star got out of line once too often. *The Sisters* concerns the lives of three sisters from Montana at the time of Teddy Roosevelt's presidency. Two of the sisters marry for money. Bette as Louise follows her heart and runs off with a newspaper reporter who suffers from an inability to settle down. He drinks then runs away. She finds herself in the middle of the San Francisco earthquake, praying that Frank is still alive and settles down in the rubble to wait for him. He shows up and they live happily ever after . . . probably in Mill Valley.

Litvak was another of those totalitarian directors, not a graduate of the Michael Curtiz school but a full professor with tenure. To make part of the earthquake scenes right he trapped the floor and some walls, put Bette on her mark and let rip. The world came tumbling down around her. She did the scene because she refused to show Litvak she was afraid, a trait which runs right through her career. She simply refused to show fear. But this time she should have thought twice. Litvak had so cleverly rigged the set that had she been just a few steps off her mark, the story of her career might have ended on this page.

"*The Sisters* will bring additional laurels to Miss Davis as a dramatic actress," *Variety* wrote. And *Hollywood Reporter* said, "Bette Davis adds still another triumph to her already long list of screen achievements. There is no doubt about the fact that she is the first lady of the screen. Her acting is a joy."

By now she really was "the first lady of the screen," and 1939 was her year to prove it once and for all. She started it with a nomination for the Academy Award. Her competition was Fay Bainter, Wendy Hiller, Norma Shearer and Margaret Sullivan. Bette went in the favourite and came out the winner. It was a fitting way to begin the year.

Her first film for 1939 was one she had tried to raise interest in for many years. *Dark Victory* was, as Jack Warner saw it, "the story about a girl who dies." He couldn't believe anyone would want to see it. But Bette managed to convince one of the studio's line producers, David Lewis and together they talked Edmund Goulding into the idea. He was willing to direct it if the Warners agreed. To keep Bette out of their hair they agreed. They bought the film from Selznick and let Casey Robinson do the screenplay. The cast consisted of Bette, George Brent, Geraldine Fitzgerald, Humphrey Bogart and a fellow who got under-the-title billing so many times that he quit show business to try another job, Ronald Reagan.

Bette played Judith Traherne and it remains one of her all-time favourite parts. She is a spoiled, rich girl who suddenly develops a serious illness. Her days are numbered, but to make them happy ones she marries her doctor, played by Brent. As he is about to go off one day she suffers an attack but hides it from him. He leaves her, not knowing as the audience does, that it will be the last time he sees her alive. The fact that he doesn't know is their victory over the dark. And as the music comes up, she climbs the stairs to her bedroom where she knows she will die.

The audience cried their eyes out and the whole story is so sad that it might even have brought a lump to Jack Warner's throat. He certainly must have felt something because when it came time to release the film, the publicity he approved was astonishing. "Out of the blazing fires of her genius," the ads. proclaimed, "the screen's most gifted actress has created a gallery of unforgettable women. Now Bette Davis, the winner of two Academy Awards, comes to you in the climax of all her dramatic triumphs." Never before had anyone at Warners even hinted that the boss felt quite so strongly about her.

The critics followed suit. "Miss Davis is superb," wrote the *New York Times*. *New Yorker Magazine* claimed, "Miss Davis is never so assured in the display of her talent." *Time Magazine* said Bette's performance put her in line for another Academy

Award. And James Shelley Hamilton, writing in the National Board of Review Magazine felt that Bette "Has never before seemed to be so entirely inside a part with every mannerism and physical aspect of her suited to its expression. If she has deserved medals before in parts of more dramatic validity, she deserves the prayerful gratitude of *Dark Victory*'s authors for putting life into something that must have looked pretty impossible on paper."

In an interview years after the film, Bette herself confessed, "Judy Traherne is what I'm like. She was 98% me."

In a much more revealing interview, Geraldine Fitzgerald who played the part of Judy's secretary Ann, opened the window on a long time Bette Davis myth. She said that before production began, some friends warned her about Bette. They said that Bette was only interested in getting her face on camera. "They said you must watch out all the time. If she smiles at you, if her character smiles at your character, she's only trying to dazzle you so you won't notice that you're in the dark. If her character walks towards your character, it's because she's going to get in front of you with the camera. Above all, if her character extends a friendly hand to you or catches you by the shoulders, it isn't her character being friendly to your character, she's turning you away from the camera." That's what Geraldine Fitzgerald said she was told and it seemed to her that the only way she could defend herself from Bette was to, "Look for a piece of furniture in the scene and somehow get yourself wedged behind it so she can't move you around." A lot of that was obviously said tongue in cheek but the idea of Bette being some sort of demon was the reputation that followed her. In some ways it still does. Geraldine Fitzgerald, like most actors and actresses who have heard those stories about Bette, was terrified to meet her. Like most actors and actresses who finally work with her, she found the rumours far from the truth. "Bette Davis was the most positive feature in my career."

The film that followed *Dark Victory* was *Juarez*, an as-close-as-possible historical representation of Benito Juarez's revolution against Maximilian and Carlotta in nineteenth century Mexico. Paul Muni starred with William Dieterle directing a John Huston screenplay which took over two years to write. One of the better 'costume' epics, it had nearly twelve hundred actors and actresses filling out the cast and an Erich Wolfgang Korngold 'period' score. Orry-Kelly dressed the cast and he must have had a field day. Unfortunately for Bette, he designed such elaborate costumes for her that at times she simply couldn't move. She lost weight and at one point passed out because of the tightness of her costume and the heat of the day. Because Carlotta eventually goes mad, Orry-Kelly started her in white clothes and gradually darkened them until the end when Carlotta, dressed in black, goes completely mad. Today the picture looks very dated but that's because film technique has changed so much and the problems of shooting on location with such a huge cast were enormous. The most interesting feature of this film has got to be the editing as Dieterle actually shot two different films and then put them together. One film involved Maximilian and Carlotta . . . portrayed by Brian Aherne and Bette . . . the other concerned Muni as Juarez. As Juarez never meets Maximilian on camera Muni didn't have to do any work until Bette and Aherne had wound up theirs. According to Bette, Muni showed up for work with fifty extra pages of script which he wanted to add to his part and being perhaps the biggest star in the Warner stable at the time, Hal Wallis let him get away with it. Bette wrote in her autobiography, "The length of any picture must be limited. When the Juarez part of the film was finished we were in trouble lengthwise. Something had to go." What went was from Bette's and Brian Aherne's part. "Mr. Muni's seniority proved our downfall." Further confusion in what actually did happen might come from the fact that once the picture was made and a final version put together, it was ordered recut with entire sequences dropped to make it less of a burden for an audience to sit through. Still, the *Los Angeles Times* called it, "One of the most pretentious films offered at any time."

Still suffering the strain of *Juarez*, she immediately began work on *The Old Maid*, an Edith Wharton story, based on the Zoe Atkins play. Edmund Goulding directed

... Bette liked that ... but her supporting actress was Miriam Hopkins, which she didn't like. They had met years before, in the Rochester theatre days, but now there seemed to be a great deal of professional friction between them. Miriam Hopkins had played *Jezebel* on Broadway and it's only natural that she should have thought of it as hers. Bette's winning the Academy Award for it obviously didn't sit well with Hopkins. Then there was Anatole Litvak. Bette says Hopkins was jealous and thought Bette and Litvak were having an affair. Hopkins played Delia, cousin to Bette's Charlotte. Originally cast as Clem was Humphrey Bogart but he was pulled off the film and George Brent brought in. Set during the Civil War, Charlotte gives birth to an illegitimate child who is then raised by Delia. Until the last reel of this old-fashioned tear jerker Charlotte is relegated to being the child's old maid aunt. The plot is entirely based on the competition between the two women for the love of one child. Perc Westmore's make-up aged Charlotte and the personal differences between Bette and Miriam Hopkins lent some reality to the picture's tension. The reviews were favourable, most of them paying special attention to Bette. "A poignant and wise performance," said the *New York Times*. "This is one of Bette Davis' outstanding pictures," said *Picturegoer*. When Miriam Hopkins' name was mentioned, in magazines like *Time* and *Life*, it was usually in the context of the off-screen feelings that the two women had for each other. The press, always eager to make headlines with such things, was quite happy to play up their rivalry.

At the outset of her next film, neither the titles or the leading man did much for her blood pressure. For a while the film was to be *Essex and Elizabeth*, giving her second billing. For a few weeks it was either to be *The Lady and The Knight* ... which Bette points out is a play on words with night ... or *The Knight and The Lady* .. which still gave her second billing. Whichever, Bette didn't approve. When Warner and Wallis cast Errol Flynn as Essex she was all the more unhappy. She was campaigning for Laurence Olivier, who, as a matter of fact, would probably have been sensational in the part and might have made this film one of the all-time greats. As it stands, Flynn preferred smiling at the camera instead of acting and proves himself to be an arrogant, talentless, wooden actor. Too bad, because Bette as Elizabeth is fantastic.

The final title was *The Private Lives of Elizabeth and Essex*. Michael Curtiz directed and again Orry-Kelly designed the costumes. As Essex vows his love for his queen, fights with her, rebels against her, revows his love, double-crosses her and eventually loses his head at the block, Bette brings to life a woman twice her age. She shaved half her head and eyebrows to give herself Elizabeth's face. She fidgets and frets and changes speeds at every turn. She cackles a laugh and instantly gets nasty. She yells then snaps back with another cackling laugh. She shows the aging queen as frustrated, discontent, confused and deeply in love with a younger man whom she can't manage to control or trust. The supporting cast included Olivia de Havilland, Donald Crisp, Alan Hale and Vincent Price as Sir Walter Raleigh. Nanette Fabray made a brief appearance under the name she used then, Nanette Fabares. There is pagentry and majesty and, best of all, Bette Davis turning in a performance that is even today, wonderful to watch.

In the *New York Times* review of the film, Frank Nugent comments that the original title of the film was *Elizabeth The Queen* and that was changed at the insistence of Errol Flynn who felt he was also star enough to be billed. It's not certain that Nugent is correct although the film was based on a Maxwell Anderson play of that title which might account for this confusion. In any case, this was a Technicolor film which Nugent called, "Stately, rigorously posed ..." and felt that it was "good enough as it stands but would have been a lot straighter if Mr. Flynn could uphold his share of it. Bette Davis' Elizabeth is a strong, resolute, glamourskimping characterization against which Mr. Flynn's Essex has about as much chance as a beanshooter against a tank." Not surprisingly, in an interview with the *Washington Post* in 1974 Bette came straight out with her opinion that Flynn, "Was not a very good actor and everything in his book about me is a lie, like how I hit him in the face with my jewelry. He was difficult for me to work with since he did not have the same dedication as an

With George Brent and Geraldine Fitzgerald in Dark Victory — *one of her favourite roles.*

Between takes on the set of The Private Lives Of Elizabeth And Essex *with Olivia de Havilland.*

actor that I had as an actress. I recall when I was playing Queen Elizabeth, I would sit there on the throne and the doors would fling open and I'd say to myself, 'Oh please God, let it be Sir Laurence Olivier'."

Immediately following that film Bette headed east for a vacation. The Warners might have had other plans for her but she wasn't going to listen to anyone. The Academy Awards were announced in February 1940 and she lost out to Vivien Leigh in *Gone With The Wind*. But that year she won the very first Redbook Magazine award for her 1939 films, and columnist Ed Sullivan named her "Queen of the Movies", with Mickey Rooney as "King". That was also the year someone referred to her as "The fourth Warner brother". She spent nearly six months in all taking a rest and putting her personal life back in order before finally thinking about another film. Several titles were suggested but all of them were flatly turned down. She settled on *All This And Heaven Too*, the screen version of a Rachel Field novel and the role of Henriette Deluzy Desportes. Set in 1841, Henriette becomes governess to the children of the Duke and Duchess de Preslin, played by Charles Boyer and Barbara O'Neill. The Duchess suspects her husband of having an affair with Henriette and makes such a to-do about it that he murders her. Henriette is named as accomplice but permitted to go free when the Duke makes a deathbed confession. On the set, she found Boyer very attractive, but Anatole Litvak who directed, very embarrassing. Their relationship was strained, obviously thanks to Miriam Hopkins' influence. Litvak was the one who actually walked away with the best reviews.

Wyler was her next director. *The Letter* was her next film. Based on a Somerset Maugham story, this was the second shot she had at a Maugham character. The first time was Mildred in *Of Human Bondage*. This time it was Leslie Crosbie, a planter's wife in Malaya who shoots and kills her lover in the opening minute of the picture then spends the next ninety-four weaving a web of deceit to escape prosecution. In the end, after the umpteenth shot of the full moon . . . there seemed to be dozens of them that month because every evening she went out, there was another moon moving behind clouds . . . she is killed by her dead lover's Oriental wife. Howard Koch wrote the screenplay and while this isn't *Casablanca*, he does have a feeling for romantic settings. Wyler used the device of Leslie's lace needle work to show how her deception becomes more and more complicated. It comes off as trite these days but it works better than all those shots of the moon! The film's title refers to a letter Leslie had written to her lover which is proof of her motive for murder. Gale Sondergaard played the lover's widow and not only looked Oriental but also had a sinister aura. Herbert Marshall played Bette's husband and he shows grief by holding his head in his hands. There is also a lot of hugging after every confession. James Stephenson plays the lawyer who defends Bette and does it with great cool. The young man playing his personal assistant, however, had seen too many Charlie Chan movies and really hams up the "number one son" act. Despite that, Wyler's direction is good and he shared most of the reviews with Bette. "The star was never better in a role that called on every ounce of her ability," the *Hollywood Reporter* said of Bette. They also approved of Wyler's work but not nearly as strongly as the *New York Times*. "The ultimate credit for as taut and insinuating a melodrama as has come along this year, a film which extenuates tension like a grim inquisitor's rack, must be given to Mr. Wyler. His hand is patent throughout."

Three months after it was released, Bette was again nominated for an Academy Award but this time she lost to Ginger Rogers who starred in *Kitty Foyle*. Both *All This And Heaven Too* and *The Letter* were on the Academy's list for Best Film awards and whilst neither won, at least the Warners were coming to understand that putting Bette with directors as strong and talented as Litvak and Wyler was proving to be a successful formula. Following these two films with one directed by Edmund Goulding therefore seemed like the right idea. She and British born Goulding did a total of four films together and in each of them she played sympathetic characters. In *The Great Lie* she plays Maggie who adopts another woman's child because it was fathered by the man who broke her heart. Bette supposedly wasn't too crazy about the script

With her sister Barbara.

The Letter *with Gale Sondergaard.*

when she first saw it but she got along well with Goulding. Lenore Coffee, who wrote the original screenplay, was willing to rework it. George Brent played the male lead and Mary Astor, at Bette's insistance, got the second female role. No awards came to Bette or Goulding for the film but Mary Astor won the Best Supporting Actress prize. It was Astor's eighty-sixth film. She was praised by the critics, as was Goulding's directing job and, of course, Bette. But the plot was a little on the thin side so that the *New York Times* suggested, except for the acting and directing, "It hardly seems worthwhile."

When she saw her next script, *The Bride Came C.O.D.* she feared it might be the same. In this "non-sensical" comedy, as she called it, Bette was teamed with Jimmy Cagney again and director William Keighley. Bette plays an oil heiress who finds herself trapped in a ghost town desert with Cagney portraying a cocky pilot. Whilst almost all the critics agreed that the result was less than hilarious, many of them thought it was sometimes funny. Bette seemed just as happy to move on to her next project, one that earned her yet another nomination for the Academy Award.

Sam Goldwyn had a property he wanted to make and Bette was the actress he wanted to make it with. That must have tasted fairly sweet to Bette, seeing as how Goldwyn himself had turned her down when he saw her very first screen test a dozen years before. Now he was supposedly willing to pay the Warners the sum of $385,000 to borrow her services, a deal Jack and his brothers couldn't turn down as they were only paying her a weekly salary in the $4000 range. The film was the screen version of Lillian Hellman's play *The Little Foxes,* with Hellman doing the script and Dorothy Parker supplying additional dialogue. Making the project all the more interesting for Bette, Goldwyn had managed to hire William Wyler as director. Bette wanted to play her role with much the same force Tallulah Bankhead had used on Broadway to first create the character of Regina but Wyler had other ideas. He saw Regina Giddens in a more toned down way. The two fought about it to the point where Bette, for the first time in her life, stormed off the set and stopped production. When Goldwyn found her he told her in no uncertain terms that if she didn't return to work she would be open to legal action. She came back but has always felt that her toned down performance was not what it could have been. The story is one that deals with greed. Herbert Marshall played the role of Horace, Regina's invalid husband. Her brothers . . . Charles Dingle played Ben, Carl Benton Reid played Oscar . . . offer her a business deal if she can convince Horace to put up the money. When Horace refuses, she quite deliberately drives him to his death, only to find out that her brothers have tricked her. Much to Bette's surprise, considering all the battles with Wyler over her characterization, the film turned out to be a masterpiece and today easily stands out as one of the best films from the period both for Bette and for Wyler. Her performance is extremely regal. She creates a high level of bitchiness early on and sustains it throughout the film. At one point, for instance, during an after-dinner piano recital in the film's first reel, Ben Hubbard stirs his coffee too loudly, so Regina kicks him. Much like he did with Julie in *Jezebel* who used her riding crop to lift her skirts, Wyler used a simple gesture to show the relationship between two of his characters. He used a lengthy close-up of another gesture to show the depth of Regina's avarice, and this particular shot is truly a classic.

Regina and Horace have discussed the possibility of putting money into her brothers' scheme with Horace saying no. She argues with him and in the tension he suffers an attack. When he spills his medicine he asks her to go upstairs to get more. She simply sits where she is. He begs. She won't move. He struggles to make his way to the stairs. She knows his money will come to her after his death. The only way to save his life is to help him upstairs. As he struggles in vain to climb them, Wyler puts the camera on Bette's face watching him out of the corner of her eyes. His direction and her acting make for a thoroughly spellbinding few minutes of film and few close-ups with such little movement have ever been so effective.

The public raved and so did the critics. "Flawless and fascinating," said the *New York Herald Tribune.* "It charts a whole new course of motion picture making." And

As Regina Giddens in The Little Foxes.

the *New York Times* agreed by noting, "*The Little Foxes* leaps to the front as the most bitingly sinister picture of the year and as one of the most cruelly realistic character studies yet shown on the screen."

But the film had taken its toll. She couldn't convince herself that her performance had been a good enough one, she and Wyler would never work together again and her health was not the best. When she asked Jack Warner to cast her in a supporting role for the film *King's Row,* he turned her down. Earlier that year she had married for the second time but her new husband Arthur Farnsworth was working for a firm in Minnesota. She broke down. When the studio needed her for a new picture she hoped she would be playing opposite John Barrymore. With great concern for her well being, they rushed her back to work. Without great concern for her artistic sense, they cast her opposite Monty Woolley.

End of the Warner Years

DURING THE '30s and up to December 1941, Bette was always considered by Japanese movie-goers their favourite actress. She was a smash in Tokyo. They thought she was wonderful because, more than any actress at the time, she represented the admirable principle of self-sacrifice. Whether or not they got to see *The Man Who Came To Dinner* before the war is a minor point, but once again . . . this time in a comedy . . . Bette played a woman of self-sacrifice. As Maggie, personal secretary to Sheridan Whiteside, she found herself working in a film that wasn't turning out the way she had originally hoped. It was her idea that Warners buy the rights to Monty Woolley's Broadway hit. But it was also her idea that she would star in it with John Barrymore. When he tested for the part he kept fluffing his lines and couldn't even get them correct off cue cards. The Warners said he'd never do but Bette argued with them. "I told them I'd rather take Barrymore's ad libbing than work with anybody else," she said years later in an interview. "I thought Woolley was pretty monotonous in the part. But can't you just see what a sensational Sheridan Whiteside Barrymore would have been. A classic part."

The perennial "senior class play" in high schools across America, the entire story is based on one gag. A famous man is invited to a wealthy couple's house for dinner, slips and falls, and must remain at the house to recuperate. Being famous, and therefore powerful, he takes over everyone's life. When he finally gets better, just as he is leaving, he slips and falls again. . . . William Keighley directed and Ann Sheridan played the part of actress Lorraine Sheldon. Jimmy Durante also makes a guest appearance. But as Bette said in *Mother Goddam*, "I felt the film was not directed in a very imaginative way. For me it was not a happy film to make. That it was a success, of course, did make me happy. I guess I never got over my disappointment in not working with the great John Barrymore."

Her next project didn't work too happily either. John Huston directed, Ernest Haller handled the camera work, Orry-Kelly designed the costumes, Perc Westmore did the make-up and Max Steiner wrote the music. Howard Koch penned the screenplay and the cast included George Brent, Olivia de Havilland and Dennis Morgan. The problems with *In This Our Life* was that Bette was miscast, her health was still fragile, Jack Warner was angry at her for having run off to Minnesota to visit her husband, Arthur Farnsworth and further hated her hair style and her wardrobe. Besides that, Olivia de Havilland and she had temporarily fallen out. Huston was in love with de Havilland so he spent a good part of the film concentrating on her, the script didn't live up to the brilliance of the book and her make-up was wrong.

She played a girl named Stanley, a role too young for her, who is pursued by the richest man in town, played by Charles Coburn. She, however, plans to marry Craig, played by George Brent, but three days before the wedding runs off with Peter, played by Dennis Morgan who just happens to be the husband of her sister Roy, played by de Havilland. Not only was the result a box-office failure but it was also a mediocre picture. The critics said so, Bette said so and then they all went about their business.

Her business was a film called *Now, Voyager* and although she didn't have Ernest Haller this time to photograph her, she did have Orry-Kelly, Max Steiner, Perc Westmore and a screenplay by Casey Robinson. Irving Rapper directed the film . . . it was supposed to be Michael Curtiz but he felt there wasn't enough action in it for him . . . and the story was based on a novel by Olive Higgins Prouty. It was originally to have been a vehicle for Irene Dunne, but when Bette saw the script she went to Wallis and asked for the role of Charlotte

Bette c. 1941.

Vale. Dunne would have to be brought in from Columbia and Bette Davis was not only interested but also on contract, so on one of those rare occasions Jack Warner gave in without a fight. Paul Henreid was cast to play the romantic lead of Jerry Durance and Claude Rains played Dr. Jaquith, the psychiatrist who helps turn Charlotte from an ugly duckling into a swan. In a sense it's a love story . . . Charlotte and Jerry meet on a cruise . . . but in the end it's something else. When they part, they do so not as a man and a woman who have been in love but as two voyagers who had come together briefly on their way to somewhere else. Whitney Stine called the plot "lachrymose" and other reviewers said that it was "more sentimental than the true psychological study it might have been". But everyone agreed on Bette's performance. "A perfect choice for the role," said *Variety* and Charles Higham summed it up by saying, "*Now, Voyager* is, of course, a camp classic, a masterpiece of schmaltz. The movie provided a wish-fulfillment fantasy for millions of women during the war years."

Many books rate the picture the best of 1942 and one of the all-time greats. Max Steiner won an Academy Award for the score and Bette was nominated for the fifth consecutive year for a Best Actress award although the prize went to Greer Garson for *Mrs. Miniver.*

Again Bette triumphed and again it was as if the studio's front office hadn't read the papers. Looking back at this particular period of her career, one which is often called her greatest, it is absolutely unbelievable that she had to fight Warner every step along the way. When Bette had finished *Now, Voyager,* she put in a bid for *Ethan Frome,* only to be told that Ida Lupino had been chosen for the starring role. The argument that Lupino might have been better suited for the part was probably a sound one, except that Jack Warner had bought the script expressly for Bette!

It was 1943 and the war was on. Bette and John Garfield founded the Hollywood Canteen to help servicemen in the Los Angeles area and during that time she made two films which must be called "war effort efforts". *Thank Your Lucky Stars* was a war time musical about a bunch of actors and actresses who put on a war time musical. Bette sang and danced. So did Dinah Shore. It's easy to tell who is who. The other, made a year later, was called *Hollywood Canteen.* Bette played Bette Davis who ran the canteen's entertainment and served meals. Nearly fifty Warner stars showed up. The best part of it is Roy Rogers and Trigger. In fact the film was so terrible that even some servicemen objected. Despite both films, the Allies won.

Much more important was the picture she made in 1943 about a German family who has fled to middle class America. As a Broadway play, *Watch On The Rhine* was a big hit for Lillian Hellman. It starred Paul Lukas who was brought to the West Coast to recreate his part of Kurt Muller. Bette played his wife Sara and was not the lead as most of the action centres on him. She took the part because she believed in the message of the play as an anti-fascist propaganda tool. Living in the Washington, D.C. area, Muller controls an anti-Nazi underground movement in Europe. Threatened with exposure to the Nazi underground in America, he kills the Count de Brancovis, played by George Coulouris. Realizing that he is needed in Europe, he bids farewell to his wife and three children and sets off on what everyone knows will be a one way trip to Germany to help underground members imprisoned by the Nazis. The screenplay was mostly written by Dashiell Hammett, Lillian Hellman's live-in friend. She added a few additional scenes to the story in the adaptation. The transition from stage to screen worked well and almost all the papers gave it high marks. The *New York Times* said, "It is the first Hollywood film to go deeply into the fundamental nature of fascism". Bette's performance was not award winning but Paul Lukas' got him the Academy Award. The film doesn't really hold up today because its message is rather laboured. Audiences today are more sophisticated and don't need to be hit over the head with a message. In those days a film charged with such emotion when America was so deeply involved in the war couldn't help but be a success.

Other emotions came into play for *Old Acquaintance.* Recently remade by George Cukor with Jacqueline Bisset and Candice Bergen, as *Rich and Famous,* this version starred Bette and Miriam Hopkins. Vincent Sherman directed but only just. It was supposed to have been Edmund Goulding, but he was pulled off the picture to do a film with Joan Fontaine and Charles Boyer. It was supposed to have starred any number of other women, like Margaret Sullivan, Janet Gaynor or Constance Bennett, except that someone in the front office decided the role of Millie was perfect for Miriam Hopkins and then as long as they couldn't figure out who'd play Kit, they might as well use Bette. It was supposed to have been a film photographed by Tony Gaudio, the cameraman who worked with Bette on *The Letter* except that Bette wanted Sol Polito who had photographed her in *Now, Voyager* and she held out until Polito was assigned to the film. It was supposed to have been a good picture, except that Sherman couldn't handle Bette or Miriam or the rivalry between the two women. Kit, a best selling authoress, returns to her home town to visit her childhood friends. Jealous of Kit's success, Millie writes a book which Kit manages to have published and Millie becomes rich and famous too. With John Loder and Gig Young providing the romantic interest, Kit must eventually give up the man she loves because Millie's daughter loves him too. In the end Millie decides to write a book about her friendship with Kit as the two women move into middle age. Except for the moments when Kit and Millie scream at each other and even slap each other around, the film doesn't go very far. But those moments of high emotion between the two old friends isn't all bad, especially when you know what the two thought of each other in real life. James Agee, writing in *The Nation* felt, "On the screen, such trash can seem, even, mature and adventurous". And the *Hollywood Reporter* likened the film to the sort of romantic drama often found in women's slick magazines.

At the end of the summer 1943, tragedy struck Bette's life. Arthur Farnsworth died of a blood clot on the brain after a fall. She had just begun preliminary work on her new picture *Mr. Skeffington* when her husband's death stopped her short. She went back East for a while and for the very first time in their relationship, Jack Warner told her to stay there until she felt ready to return to work. Bette says she was deeply touched by his understanding. In *The Lonely Life* she describes her character at that period. "In those years I made many enemies. I was a legendary terror; I had my fine Italian hand in everything. Thirty-five is the age for a woman in my opinion. Oh, to stay thirty-five forever. When I was my most unhappy I lashed out rather than whined. I was aggressive but curiously passive. I had to be in charge but I didn't want to be. I was hated, envied and feared and I was more vulnerable than anyone would care to believe. It wasn't difficult to discover that when people disliked me they really detested me. And they couldn't do any more about me than they could about death and taxes. I must have been a frustration to many."

When she came back to Hollywood, having buried Arthur Farnsworth in New England, she tried to bury herself in work. Her activities at the Hollywood Canteen kept her busy some of the time and *Mr. Skeffington* the rest of it. A difficult film to make, Bette as Fanny Trellis is required to age twenty-six years during the story. At the beginning of the film, she is "the beauty of New York" whose brother, played by Richard Waring, is something of a rake. His gambling debts have become a bother to his banker Job Skeffington, played by Claude Rains, who comes to see Fanny about the problem. More out of family loyalty than love she marries him. The brother goes off to World War I and gets himself killed. She blames Job for her brother's death, the rift in their marriage widens and they divorce. Fanny takes their daughter, plus a large cash settlement from Job, and starts to live her own life again. But as her daughter, played by Marjorie Riordan, grows up Fanny convinces the girl to go off to live with her father. Fanny's social life is a whirlwind affair. Then, when the daughter reaches eighteen and World War II is about to break out, Job sends the girl back to her mother who is in the midst of a love affair with a younger man named Johnny. Fanny suddenly contracts diptheria and although she eventually recovers, it costs her a great deal. Her good looks fade and her hair falls out. Johnny then runs off with Fanny's daughter. Now faced with old age and ugliness, everything seems black for Fanny until Job comes back into her life. He too is old and blind so he cannot tell how she looks. Vincent Sherman directed as best he could. Perc Westmore's make-up aged Bette in such a memorable way that her make-up and her acting in this film immediately gave birth to a characterization of Bette Davis that is so often mimicked by male actors in drag. It was probably right here that the gay community discovered the Bette Davis character that is so often impersonated. And the *Los Angeles Times* made a point of playing on just this in their review. "The mimics will have more fun than a box of monkeys imitating Bette Davis as Fanny Skeffington, née Trellis. Excellently portraying a light, selfish woman in her latest feature, the Academy Award winning actress of other years attains as definite a characterization as she has ever proffered. It is just the kind of enactment to inveigle the travesty specialists."

Based on a book by an English novelist who signed her work simply "Elizabeth", Ernest Haller photographed the film and Orry-Kelly designed some forty costumes. Produced by Philip and Julius Epstein, Jack Warner paid particular attention to this film since there are a great deal of what might be called "Jewish themes". Job Skeffington is Jewish . . . eventually a victim of Nazi oppression . . . and to make certain that unflattering stereotypes and the usual prejudices didn't slip into the film, the powers that be watched closely. The Epsteins wrote the screenplay, and according to Bette, throughout the shooting notes would come from the front office suggesting additional dialogue to make Job Skeffington look like a saint. Luckily better sense prevailed. Bette and Claude Rains managed to fight off a reverse-stereotype and turn out a fine product. On the other hand, the film was done in black and white and that was something of a disappointment to Bette who had fought to have it done in colour. Throughout the film there is a running gag which is, if nothing else, good fun. Fanny is forever breaking dates with her friend Janie Clarkson. They never manage to meet when they planned to and because of that the character is never seen on the screen. Bette received her seventh Best Actress nomination for her work but the prize went to Ingrid Bergman for *Gaslight*.

It doesn't appear that this film was a particularly happy one. Bette supposedly spent a great deal of time fighting with the Epsteins and trying to add lines to her role which she felt would give more to Fanny's personality. The result was an incident that must be a Hollywood first. The Epsteins walked off their own film. They reportedly felt that there wasn't anything they could do as long as Bette Davis was the film's director. Also, a number of minor incidents took place on the set including differences between Bette and Vincent Sherman about the rubber mask which Perc Westmore had modelled for Fanny's later years. Everyone who worked with her on that film has at one time or another said that Bette was especially difficult, although her husband's death makes her irritability a little more understandable.

One incident on the set has never been explained, except by saying that it was hopefully an unintentional accident. Her eyewash had been switched for an acid that nearly blinded her in one eye. If Perc Westmore hadn't been standing near her when she used the eyewash and promptly washed her eye it may have been too late to save it. As it was she was under treatment for a few weeks by a specialist.

The picture came in sixty days late, over budget, and not having won Bette a lot of friends. The Epsteins tried to get their name off the credits and didn't speak to Bette for years. Vincent Sherman never worked with her again. The *New York Times* panned her outright. Jack Warner complained about her at every turn. And finally Bette went to him asking to be let out of her contract. He, of course, refused.

She then married William Grant Sherry, a Sunday painter eight years her junior, and right from the start most of her biographers report that the marriage didn't look as though it would last. She had already begun work on her next film, *The Corn Is Green* and it turned out to be one of her classics. Based on the Emlyn Williams play, in which Ethel Barrymore had starred on Broadway and Sybil Thorndike in London, the film's screenplay was by Casey Robinson with Irving Rapper directing. Lilly Moffat takes up teaching school in a small Welsh mining town opposed by most of the townsfolk. The children, they feel, should be in the mines, not a classroom. Thwarted at every step, she is just about ready to give up when she realizes that one of her students,

As Charlotte Vale in Now, Voyager *with Paul Henreid.*

In Mr. Skeffington *with Philip Reed.*

played by John Dall, has genius. She dedicates her efforts to pushing him, sometimes much too hard, to prepare for his entrance exams to Oxford. When he learns he has fathered a child he wants to give up his studies and go back to the mines but Miss Moffat agrees to raise the baby as if it were her own so the boy can return to school.

Again, the storyline has become so clichéd over the years because every television western series has used it at least once a season. But the role of Miss Moffat was one she would come back to years later. Playing an older woman required Perc Westmore's help and he provided a make-up that aged her a good ten years. Her dresses were padded to make her look fatter and then, towards the end of the second week of shooting, she decided she needed a wig. It had been suggested right from the start, but she turned it down, preferring to have her own hair styled. Rapper now said it was too late, but she insisted and he supposedly said to one of his production assistants, "What she needs is a psychiatrist, not a director". She continued to fight for the wig until everyone decided to test her with it and let Jack Warner decide. Seeing the tests he announced that the wig would stay and that, despite the costs, those two weeks already in the can would be reshot. A lucky decision for Bette since the heavy wig saved her life. She was shooting a scene when a light cover fell or might even have been pushed, from the ceiling. It hit her and had she not been wearing the wig, the accident could have been fatal. As it was, she suffered severe headaches for the next few days which held up production.

The entire movie was shot on a sound stage and because it was the film version of a play, she had insisted that it all be filmed in dramatic order. Movies are almost never done that way and because of her accident, production had to stop. Shooting around her would have upset that dramatic order. As it was, filming that way created problems dealing with the changes in a bulky set. They couldn't do the interiors, strike them and then build the exteriors. They had to go back and forth following the script. The set required several tons of dirt for the roads and fields, grass sod and even snow. There were wind machines and clouds that floated by and fog that came in off the hills. There were also goats that grazed in the middle of the set.

When the picture was released the studio did a strange thing. Perhaps because the role of the school teacher was something different for Bette, the Warner advertising people used lines like, "In her heart of hearts, she could never hold him," suggesting that the teacher/student relationship was sexual. "You should have seen the ad. I stopped," Bette told the *Washington Post*. "That showed Miss Moffat practically naked. These ads. were a real hoax to the public. The studios always tried to suggest that period movies were modern sex shows because they were afraid people wouldn't go to period movies. I used to say to Jack Warner, 'If you think the public won't go to costume movies, why do you make them? Why weren't you frightened about what could happen at the box-office when you planned the production?' Of course, you never got a sensible answer because the thing couldn't be made to make sense."

The reviews were excellent. The *Picture Post* wrote that only Bette Davis, "Could have combatted so successfully the obvious intention of the adapters of the play to make frustrated sex the mainspring of the chief character's interest in the young miner." The *New York Herald Tribune* felt, "Bette Davis gives a sharp, vital interpretation of Miss Moffat." They also said that with collaborators such as Casey Robinson and Irving Rapper, "plus Bette Davis to give dignity to the central role among an excellent supporting cast, a fine play has been passed through the Warner Brothers studio and become a polished motion picture".

In spite of the reviews, for the first time in seven years, Bette was not nominated for an Academy Award.

And in spite of the reviews for her next picture, Bette was not nominated for "Producer of the Year" either. "You know," wrote Bosley Crowther of the *New York Times* when he previewed *A Stolen Life,* both starring and produced by Bette Davis, "there are two types of characters which Miss Davis usually plays in her films. The good girls, long suffering and selfless. And the bad girls, inclined to spite and greed. Well, the lady here gives us both varieties, with the mechanical aid of trick photography, and the illusion is more optical than dramatic when the two are together on the screen."

Bette played identical twins, Kate and Patricia, with Glenn Ford as Bill, the main love interest. Dane Clark, Charles Ruggles and Walter Brennan all had supporting roles. The storyline goes like this. Kate falls for Bill but Bill has fallen for Patricia. The two get married and plan to head for South America. Kate retreats to Cape Cod. But at the last minute, Patricia doesn't go with Bill as their marriage is already falling apart. The two sisters rediscover each other, and spend time boating on the Cape until there is an accident and Patricia is drowned. Kate is saved by the lighthouse keeper who mistakes her for her twin and immediately wires Bill to come home. Kate then decides to deceive Bill into thinking she is Patricia. Bill comes to her, knowing all along that it is Kate he has returned to. The point is that in the end good Kate has triumphed over bad Patricia and he should have married Kate in the first place.

Cue Magazine panned the film. "A series of glib, overworked dramatic clichés that are handled as obviously and heavily as a *True Confessions* tear jerker. The sets are too slick, the costumes too smart, the lines too obviously polished and pat, and the acting too superficial." But Bette in *The Lonely Life* was not of that opinion. "*Stolen Life* turned out very well," she said. "In fact it was a big hit."

There are two things that stand out about the film.

The first is the photography. The split-screen work was far and away the best of the era. Ernest Haller and Sol Polito worked on the film together and their joint camera expertise, coupled with director Curtis Bernhardt's determination to push everyone's talents to the limit, made for some wonderful moments. Bette acts with herself and proves quite good at it. The standard way had been to play the actor on one half of the frame, blocking out the other half. Then you reroll the film, block out the first half and put the actor on the other side. In the technique used for *Stolen Life*, scenes were also shot twice, but not on the same film. Two negatives were aligned in the lab with voices dubbed on a separate track for post-production synchronization. The result was that the two Bettes can move around each other. To make the technique as perfect as possible, the camera and all of the furniture had to be nailed to the floor so that everything would always be in the exact same spot for both takes. They actually got so good at the technique that at one point Bette passes a match to herself to light a cigarette. Those few seconds, all by themselves, must rate as classic film trickery.

The second notable thing about *A Stolen Life* is that it was Bette's first and only attempt at playing Producer. She had formed a company called B. D. Inc. and come to terms with the Warners on such problems as distribution percentages. She hired people she wanted to work with, such as Haller and Polito and went about making a movie . . . only to find that being a producer wasn't exactly what she thought it would be. "They didn't really let me do it," she told the *Washington Post* in 1974. "Didn't let me have the actual say of a producer. I'd been there since I was a kid but they didn't take me seriously. It was a phoney deal. But I shouldn't have given up. There were plenty of things I wanted to change. Lots of money was wasted in lots of areas and I knew where. I'd made enough films. But it was a system that seemed proof against change."

Curtis Bernhardt, in *The Celluloid Muse* remembered Bette's work on the film differently. "Despite what she claims in her autobiography, she did not produce the picture, although it was made by her production company. I'll face her any day on that. It had in fact, no official producer."

For her next film she went back to being just one of the cast. And this time the cast was made up of the *Now, Voyager* team. The adage in Hollywood has always been to ride with a winner. So if *Now, Voyager* worked once, it might, Jack Warner hoped, work again.

It didn't.

Bette Davis, Paul Henreid and Claude Rains got together again and the story was called *Deception*. Based on Louis Verneuil's play *Jealousy*, you can guess the major theme. Christine finds Karel, played by Henreid, still alive at the end of the war.

Believing her to be the same girl he loved and left at the start of the war, he marries her. She, however, has been having a "relationship" with the composer Alexander Hollenius, played by Rains. When Hollenius threatens to expose their relationship to Karel, who happens to be a musician trying to make a come-back after years in a German prison camp, she kills Hollenius. Karel's reappearance to the music world is successful, she confesses to him that she's murdered the composer, he forgives her and promises to stand by her when justic prevails. Strangely enough, most of the reviews were favourable. Irving Rapper directed and got good marks. "Faultless," wrote *Cue Magazine*, also giving credit to Erich Wolfgang Korngold for his score and an original cello concerto which, they said, was "a classic example of what fine screen music should be like". The *New York Post* said, "The performances are rather good. Miss Davis' is one of her standard stints, powerful emotions held on a strong rein". And *PM Magazine's* reviewer Cecelia Ager said, "It's like grand opera, only the people are thinner."

There was, however, a major problem with this film. Hollywood in those days lived in fear of the Hayes Office which acted as official censor. One of the basic rules was that crimes committed on the screen had to be paid for. The classic case was Hammett's *Maltese Falcon*. At the end of the book, Sam Spade takes the law into his own hands and shoots the girl. On screen that was a no-no so, when the film was done Bogart must turn Brigid O'Shaughnessy over to the police to stand trial for murder. His killing her would mean he'd have to stand trial as well. In *Deception* evil should have won out but the final scene, where she confesses her crime, turns the hour and a half that preceded it into nonsense. Bette even says that everyone knew it and tried lots of ways to end the film, "But they were all so phoney we never did get a solution."

They didn't do very well at the box office either, despite an excellent performance by Claude Rains.

Bette followed that film by giving birth to Barbara Davis Sherry, on May 1, 1947. It was her first child and although it may have fulfilled her as a woman, it kept her off the sound stage for a year. Her relations with the Warners were hardly the best when she finished *Deception* but not working was not her style. She returned to the lot to do *Winter Meeting*. And it's too bad because she would have been better off had she not bothered.

Ethel Vance's novel of the same name was a quality book, a study of a non-Catholic named Susan and a devoted Catholic named Slick. First they fall in love then they fall out of love then they fall in love again except that Slick wants to be a priest. The test of true love comes when Susan sends Slick away to do just that. Bretaigne Windust directed and until then the most he had ever managed was working as a dialogue coach on a Ronald Reagan film. The best that anyone could say about the film was what one weekly news magazine came up with. "Bette Davis' talents are great enough to be sometimes apparent even in the midst of such unrewarding mediocrity." Jim Davis, who played Slick, had the sense years later to play Jock Ewing in *Dallas* and Bette had the sense to try another picture. "I should have been bright enough to junk it," she told an interviewer. "What a nothing it was. Having to make a great point of showing them coming out of separate bedrooms when the story is about a woman having her first affair."

June Bride was a better film, but didn't do what it should have at the box-office and suddenly Bette's career was on the skids. Bette played Linda, the editor of a woman's magazine who hires Robert Montgomery, playing Casey, on to her staff. They had been lovers before the war but he had gone off as an itinerant correspondent. He's an anti-feminist and she's the boss. He wants to write about macho stuff and she assigns him "female themes", like weddings. He not only succeeds in the assignments but in taming her too. The two go off together for the rest of their lives where he will wear the pants and she will follow faithfully.

Luckily the film was billed as a comedy. Windust directed again, faring better this time and when the reviews came in they were good. The public liked her playing comedy, the critics liked her playing comedy and she was funny when she wanted to

One of the happier moments at Warner Bros. – Jack Warner (at the top of the cake) celebrates.

be. She didn't get along with Robert Montgomery and the battling with Jack Warner continued, so none could say that this film was a happy experience. When she expected that *Ethan Frome* would be her next picture, she found herself cast in *Beyond The Forest*. King Vidor directed, which should have helped, and Lenore Coffee did the screenplay which also should have helped. But nothing did. The film was downright awful.

The plot has to do with a woman who is married to one man but willing to fall in love with another. Bette worked with Joseph Cotton playing her husband and David Brian playing her lover. When she becomes pregnant there are great discussions as to whether or not she will have the baby. When she decides not to, she induces a miscarriage by jumping off a bridge. In some parts of the country this particular two minute segment was cut out of the movie. At the end of the film she dies as the train she had hoped to be on leaves for Chicago. "One of the most unfortunate stories she has ever tackled," one reviewer said. And the *Los Angeles Examiner* felt a good part of the film's failure was Bette's fault. "The rest of the cast, all good actors, seem so dumbstruck by the antics of the star that they give the impression of merely watching from the sidelines."

There might have been some truth in what they said. People like King Vidor who wrote about Bette in his book *On Film Making*, claimed that she, "Resented my directions and unbeknown to me went to the head of the studio and told them that unless I was taken off the picture she would not appear for work the next day."

Jack Warner said no.

Probably unbeknown to both of them was the fact that her marriage with William Grant Sherry was going bad and that she was greatly concerned about the future of her child. With understandable frustration she told Warner that she would finish the picture but in exchange she wanted out of her contract.

And this time, fed up with her, Jack Warner said okay.

89

From Eve to Baby Jane

EVERYTHING HAPPENED VERY QUICKLY. It was almost as if her life was a film and someone suddenly put the projector on double-speed.

The Warner PR people sent word out that Bette was through and a few days later she filed for divorce from Sherry.

Offers for new pictures started coming in. The papers were filled with rumours. It seemed as if every studio in Hollywood had plans for her. So did every producer on Broadway. She found herself at one of those extremely dangerous points in a career. After eighteen years on a payroll she was unemployed. The reviews for *Beyond The Forest* weren't helping to make her feel secure. The temptation, when you suddenly find yourself afloat, is to grab the first thing that comes your way and hope it will save you. The smart thing to do . . . except that it's also the toughest . . . is to wait, keep afloat and make absolutely certain that it's a liferaft you're grabbing. Of course, the problem with waiting is the constant worry that the liferaft may never come.

In this case for Bette, luck was on her side.

What happened was a film called, ironically enough, *The Story Of A Divorce*. Curtis Bernhardt had written it with Bruce Manning and planned to direct it with Manning co-producing for RKO. When they heard Bette was free, they went straight for her. It was a tough script, well written and with a real-life ending which Bette accepted, playing the part of Joyce with Barry Sullivan as David. After twenty years of marriage the couple decide to divorce. Using flashbacks as cleverly as he had used the split-screen technique in *A Stolen Life,* Bernhardt shows Joyce reliving her past. First as a teenager . . . a real make-up and acting job for a woman of her age . . . and then as an adult who will stop at nothing to drive her husband on to success. But Joyce is a woman who wants her share of it and when the divorce goes through she threatens to publically expose his affair with another woman unless she is awarded most of his fortune in the settlement. For a while she lives her own life then they meet again at the daughter's marriage. David wants to try again but Joyce starts calculating, wondering if his return is worth the reconciliation.

The real-life ending was such a change from those standard Warner happy endings that it pleased her. But other things frightened her. As she told the Associated Press when she started on the picture, "I peered around the set and didn't see a familiar face. There was also a feeling of strangeness because I hadn't been before a camera in eight months. Suddenly I had a sensation I hadn't felt in years. Will they think I can act well enough. . . ."

During the final few weeks on that picture she received a call from Darryl Zanuck. He was running Twentieth Century Fox and he said he needed her. Claudette Colbert was supposed to star in a film for him, but she had hurt her back and couldn't work. Zanuck wanted to know if Bette would take the part. The last time the two switched roles it was Bette who didn't get the part in *It Happened One Night* and it was Claudette Colbert who went on to win an Academy Award for that film. This time the part was Margo Channing and the film was *All About Eve*.

"I can think of no project that from the outset was as rewarding from the first day to the last," Bette wrote in her memoires. "It was a great script, had a great director and was a cast of professionals all with parts they liked. It was a charmed production from the word go. After the picture was released, I told Joe he had resurrected me from the dead."

The Joe in question was Joe Mankiewicz and he summarised Margo's character saying she should treat a mink coat like a poncho. He had been warned about Bette's behaviour on

As Margo Channing in All About Eve.

a set and told that she would probably rewrite the entire script and refuse most of his direction. However, Mankiewicz later said he found Bette to be a director's dream as the totally prepared actress.

Mankiewicz had written the screenplay himself, based on the story *The Wisdom of Eve* by Mary Orr. He cast Ann Baxter as Eve, Hugh Marlowe as the playwright Lloyd Richards, Celeste Holm as his wife Karen, Gary Merrill as Bill and added to the cast George Sanders, Thelma Ritter . . . who is absolutely wonderful as Margo's maid Birdie . . . and Marilyn Monroe. Eddie Fisher had a bit part but it ended up on the cutting room floor. The film belongs to Margo . . . the story of an actress afraid to grow old . . . pushed by Eve who comes into her life as an admirer, takes up a post as her secretary, and then manages to use her boss as a stepping stone on her way to becoming a star. Filled with voice-overs and flashbacks, Mankiewicz doesn't just sketch Margo, he paints her in oils. Because he was a writer before he was a director, *All About Eve* is not only a wonderful motion picture, it's also a tremendously effective piece of writing. "He can't take his eyes off my legs," Margo says about Bill. He retorts, "Like a nylon lemon peel."

"Everybody has a heart," says Margo at the party. "Except some people."

Later she's told, "There's a Hollywood star out there." And Margo comes up with the throaty response, "Too bad. I just sent my autograph book to the cleaners."

George Sanders shows up at the party with Marilyn Monroe whom he introduces as a "Graduate of the Copacabana School of Dramatic Arts." He says to Margo, "You remember Miss Caswell?" She answers, "I do not. How do you do." And Marilyn replies, breathlessly, "We never met. Maybe that's why."

When she gets drunk at the party and turns on Bill, Margo makes a magnificent exit with, "You be the host. It's your party. Happy birthday. Welcome home. And we who are about to die, salute you."

Towards the end of the film George Sanders spots Margo at the Stork Club. From his table across the room, he raises his glass in toast to her. Bette takes a spring onion, toasts him with that, and while still staring at him, quickly bites the onion in half.

In the final reel of the film, once Eve's speech is made and she's accepted the drama prize, Margo says to her, "Nice speech. But I wouldn't worry too much about your heart. You can always put that award where your heart ought to be."

Yet the most stunning and absolutely the most memorable line happens at the beginning of the party scene. Peeved with her friends and especially with Bill she makes a few nasty comments. Eve says, "We know you. We've seen you like this before. Is it over or just beginning?" Margo answers by swigging her dry martini, tossing the olive back into the glass, then handing the glass to Bill. She starts to move away from them, then turns and warns, "Fasten your seat belts. It's going to be a bumpy night."

Bette won her eighth nomination for Best Actress but did not get the award. Judy Holliday won for *Born Yesterday*. On the other hand she did get Gary Merrill. The two were married that summer. As 1950 wore on, the rave reviews continued to pour in. Bette was given the New York Film Critics Circle Award and magazine articles turned her performance into a personal triumph. Some of them suggested that she had consciously modelled the part of Margo on real-life Broadway star, Tallulah Bankhead. Part of the reason seems to be that when Bette began work on the film, she was having throat problems and her voice was lower than usual making her inadvertently sounding like Bankhead. Bette has always claimed that those similarities were never created on purpose.

Bette and Gary Merrill adopted a baby girl and named her Margot. Then Howard Hughes came along and did a strange thing. *The Story Of A Divorce* had not yet been released and Hughes wanted the ending changed. Instead of Joyce sitting with David calculating how she can use him, Hughes wanted the film to end with Joyce suggesting that if David wanted to come back, he should take some time to think it over and then decide. It was a much softer ending and Bette wasn't happy. But Hughes wanted things done his way and the ending was reshot. The title was changed to *Payment On*

Demand and once again the critics thought it was wonderful. Most of them noted that if *Payment On Demand* had been held back to ride on the success of *All About Eve,* it was unnecessary because *Payment On Demand* was worthy enough to stand on it's own. The *Hollywood Reporter* said that Bette showed "The powerful range of her acting talent. It's a superb part and the actress plays superbly, reading nuances of the modern woman into it that her fans will recognize and understand." The *Los Angeles Times* said that the film and especially Bette's performance in it, actually one-upped her previous film. "This is no such flashy performance as she gave in *All About Eve.* It is much finer grained."

Riding now on two successes, Bette made a mistake. She agreed to play Janet in Douglas Fairbanks Jr.'s production of *Another Man's Poison.* Filmed in England, Gary Merrill had a role, as did Anthony Steele, Barbara Murray and Emlyn Williams. It has to do with blackmail and murder and poisoned brandy. The *Hollywood Reporter* suggested, "Plainly the director was obliged to give Miss Davis her head for the same zealous overplaying is not evident among others in the cast." The director in question was Irving Rapper and he had supposedly been hired at Bette's request. The *Hollywood Reporter* also noted that Bette, as "Queen of the vixens, combs her hair, lights cartons of cigarettes, snaps her fingers and bites her consonants, and it all adds up to a performance that you'd expect to find from a nightclub impersonation of the actress."

She had fought constantly with Rapper on the project and seemed especially glad to get home, happy to see what scripts the mail would bring. With Merrill's star rising, he accepted a major part in *Phone Call From A Stranger,* a film that starred Shelley Winters and Michael Rennie. As it was a Twentieth Century Fox affair, Bette convinced Darryl Zanuck to let her play a small role. It was very much a bit part, that of Marie Hoke, a bedridden invalid. While she obviously thought she was taking the role because it offered her an acting challenge some other people began to wonder if perhaps she was looking for work because her star was falling.

It was almost unthinkable that after eight Oscar nominations and two awards, after huge successes like *All About Eve* and *Payment On Demand,* Bette Davis would do such a minor part. One of the rumours was that she took the role because without her Zanuck would never have given Gary Merrill a part. It's a rumour that was probably based on nothing more than the general nastiness that permeates certain levels of Hollywood society.

Rumours could have become reality because her next role, as Margaret Elliot in *The Star* was all about an Academy Award winning actress who is fighting age, declining popularity and bankruptcy. Sterling Hayden played one of her former leading men and Natalie Wood played her twelve year old daughter. It's the rather depressing story of a woman who can't forget she was once a movie star, and while she can never be that again, she isn't sure that anyone who has been a movie star can ever be a woman again either. "*The Star* offers some authentic behind the scenes glimpses of movie town activities," said *Time.* "But if the scripters have not made the most of their theme, Bette Davis makes the most of her role. Her performance as an ex-first lady of the screen is first-rate." But then *Time* went a little bit further, and perhaps even inadvertantly, struck a slightly sour note. "It is a marathon one-woman show, and all in all, proof that Bette Davis, with her strident voice, nervous stride, mobile hands and popping eyes, is still her own best imitator."

It's that last line that hinted Bette might have made a mistake taking on *The Star.* She was nominated for the ninth time for an Academy Award but didn't win the prize, losing to Shirley Booth with *Come Back, Little Sheba.*

Nearly thirty months separated the opening of *The Star* and the opening of *The Virgin Queen* which marked her sixty-sixth motion picture. The papers said she preferred being a housewife. The truth was that she had certain responsibilities at home she hadn't counted on. They centred around her little girl, Margot who turned out to be mentally handicapped.

When Twentieth Century Fox sent her the script for *Sir Walter Raleigh* and asked her to play Queen Elizabeth, she must have flashed back seventeen years to her film with Errol Flynn. This time it would be a DeLuxe Colour and Cinemascope extravaganza co-starring Richard Todd, Joan Collins, Jay Robinson and Herbert Marshall.

The Virgin Queen was the title used when the film was released in mid-1955, and it basically picks up the story of the Queen's court where *The Private Lives Of Elizabeth and Essex* left off. This time though Bette is a more subdued Elizabeth. She shaved her head and eyebrows again and in some scenes wore a rubber mask to cover her hair and show the Queen as nearly bald. She always said she could associate a lot with Elizabeth I but, unlike the last time she played the part, she was not the Queen of this studio. Zanuck was boss and his big star was then Marilyn Monroe. Now when Bette complained about lighting or camera angles or what she felt was something unprofessional, she didn't carry the same weight as she did at Warners seventeen years before. It created tensions, although Hedda Hopper wrote in her column that the problems on the set were not Bette's fault. They were, she said, "With other players on the lot who wanted to spend their time watching her act. Finally they had to be barred from the set as their visits were delaying the picture."

Of course the critics loved her. *Films In Review* said, "Miss Davis' latest portrayal of Elizabeth I is better than her interpretation of that personage in *Elizabeth And Essex*." Sure, the role was absolutely hers but the picture was not what Hollywood called box office.

Backed with good reviews . . . the financial figures would take longer to come in . . . she made a pair of pictures for release in 1956. *Storm Center* was a Phoenix Production done for Columbia. *The Catered Affair* was for MGM. According to most reports they were filmed in this order although *The Catered Affair* was released first.

Originally called *The Library*, *Storm Center* was turned into a screenplay by the director, Daniel Taradash. It co-starred Brian Keith, Kim Hunter and Paul Kelly with Bette playing Alicia Hull, a librarian willing to fight the entire town to defend the principle that books on Communism should be offered on her library's shelves. The impact of the film is slightly lost these days but in 1956 the McCarthy years were still fresh in everyone's mind.

The Catered Affair was another matter. All the elements were there right from the beginning. Ernest Borgnine, Barry Fitzgerald, Debbie Reynolds and Rod Taylor filled out the cast with a bit part played by Mae Clarke. Directed by Richard Brooks, it was a Gore Vidal screenplay based on a Paddy Chayefsky play for television. Borgnine had hit it big with *Marty* so here he was trying again, this time as a cab driver in the Bronx married to Bette. The title refers to the on/off wedding reception for their daughter. The reviews seemed mixed. Some papers, like the *New York Daily News* said, "Miss Davis makes us believe that she is Mrs. Tom Hurley of The Bronx." But *The New Yorker* wasn't so sure. "Bette Davis is done up to resemble a fat and slovenly housewife but even so she conveys the impression that she's really a dowager doing a spot of slumming in the Bronx." Looking at the film today, you find a performance that she obviously loved doing. It is one of those performances which has gotten better with age. When it was first shown there were three elements that got in the way. The first was that MGM didn't seem to want to spend a lot of money pushing the film. The second was that it was released too soon after Thelma Ritter had played the same part in the Chayevsky television version. And the third was because *Storm Center* was held back for release until after *The Catered Affair*.

It was three years before she made another film. During those years she concentrated on work for television, starring in specials and making guest appearances in weekly series. She found TV in those days to be like movies had been some twenty-five years before. "We used to make six, eight pictures a year," she told the *Los Angeles Times* in 1957. "So these television schedules, rehearse two days, shoot three, don't terrify me." But she never really managed the transition from big screen to small in the way that many television stars today can't make movies. There was talk of a series or two for her but they never materialized. She was slated to do a role in the stage production of *Look Homeward Angel* but she took a bad fall and seriously hurt her back. Also, she didn't like 'live' television.

It was not a happy period in her life, so when a pair of offers came in for guest appearances in pictures being made in Europe, she jumped at them. It was not only work, it was also the chance to do some travelling. The first film was *John Paul Jones*, starring Robert Stack and directed by John Farrow. She played Catherine The Great, didn't care for Farrow but didn't have to get along with him for long. She only had a few days of shooting, and left $50,000 richer for her efforts. A week later she started work on *The Scapegoat* with Alec Guinness. It was a Gore Vidal screenplay and Bette played a wonderful character named Countess De Gue, a bed-ridden dowager who is addicted to cigars and morphine. Guinness played duel roles in this Daphne du Maurier murder mystery and some reviewers said he was "convincing", while they felt, "Bette Davis uses her three decades of acting experience to make the countess a commanding and wholly believable figure."

Back in the States she found more offers for television – she did her first western in an episode for the series *Wagon Train* – but the movie offers were still few and far between. It was tough enough in Hollywood during those days for young actresses to find film work. It was next to impossible for anyone of Bette's star status. So she worked in television then embarked on a tour across America with Gary Merrill in *The World Of Carl Sandburg*. They covered nearly seventy cities in just over four months. The show consisted of Bette and Merrill reading from collections of Sandburg's Writings. To make certain that she would look her best, she called on her old friend Orry-Kelly to design a pair of gowns for her. She looked terrific and the tour was a huge success. They got rave reviews wherever they played. Then Merrill went to film a picture and Bette headed for New England. She was going to open the show on Broadway in the fall. That summer she and Merrill were divorced. Barry Sullivan worked with her in the show for a while then Leif Erickson took over the male lead as they opened in New York. It didn't work. When Tennessee Williams approached her with his new play *The Night Of The Iguana*, she read for him and got the part of Maxine, the woman who owns the hotel. That was also about the time she agreed to write *The Lonely Life*.

Then along came Apple Annie. Frank Capra had teamed up with Glenn Ford to remake the 1933 Columbia film *Lady For A Day*. Based on a Damon Runyon story called *Madame La Gimp*, their version was called *Pocketful Of Miracles*. Capra directed and most of the action centres around Bette as Apple Annie so she might have been considered the star. But the picture was both co-produced by and starred Ford. Hope Lang was in the film, as were Ann-Margaret, Peter Falk and a wonderful selection of character actors such as Sheldon Leonard, Arthur O'Connell, Edward Everett Horton and Jerome Cowan. Unfortunately, life on the set was not pleasant. First there was a problem with the dressing rooms. Bette was assigned one next to Ford's then moved because Hope Lang wanted it. Bette might have been insulted but she moved without a fight even though it seems Ford himself was too embarrassed to ask her personally and sent an underling. On top of that, Ford gave an interview where he claimed that he had decided to offer Bette the part so she could start making a come-back because, after all, she had done him a favour by getting him a role in *A Stolen Life*. This time Bette had a fit. Near the end of the shooting, Bette was informed that her mother Ruthie had passed away. She went back East as soon as she could.

The Night Of The Iguana opened in New York in late December 1961. It won awards but she wasn't happy here either. She didn't get along with the male lead, Patrick O'Neal.

Her reviews in the play were solid, calling her, "Marvellously brash and beguiling." Those for Apple Annie were in the same vein. "Bette Davies slices the jambon in a way that will have them weeping in their lace hankies in the boondocks," wrote *Playboy*. But the *New York Daily News* came up with, "It brings Bette Davis out of semi-retirement to play the ginsoaked apple peddler, Annie, which she does to our complete satisfaction."

The key words there are "semi-retirement." Here she was, fifty-three years old, a two-time Oscar winner, a living legend in the history of the American screen and now people were talking about "semi-retirement." It must have been very frightening.

Enter Robert Aldrich. The question he wanted to ask was, *Whatever Happened to Baby Jane?* Joan Crawford said yes first. Then Bette said yes. It was the movie sleeper of 1962. A black and white low budget affair, Aldrich had peddled the idea around town and found nothing but doors closing in his face. The one that finally stayed open was Seven Arts Associates.

"My immediate problem was to get Bette Davis and Joan Crawford to make *Baby Jane* for what I could pay them, a figure far below their going salaries," Aldrich explained to the *New York Times.* He offered them a piece of the action and a small salary. But the major studios wouldn't go along. As Bette has often said, "When Aldrich tried to interest the studios in Joan Crawford and myself, the moguls said, 'We wouldn't give you a dime for those two old broads'."

Then Eliot Hyman came along from Seven Arts and Aldrich was listed as Associate Producer and Director. His biggest worry became the fact that Bette and Joan couldn't stand each other. Everyone expected a volatile set, Aldrich among them, but what they found was something quite different. As he explained, "I think it's proper to say that they really detested each other but they behaved absolutely perfectly. There was never an abrasive word in public and not once did they try to upstage each other." Instead they comported themselves like the professionals they both were and the result of it all is a memorable motion picture. Both of them can act, and for the thirty days that it took to make the film, neither of them stopped. Bette is downright terrifying as she cackles grotesquely, serving Crawford a bird for lunch, then a rat. Crawford screams in sheer horror and spins her wheelchair around in circles. They act together and react to each other, and knowing what they thought about each other, you can't help but wonder just how much of the screaming and yelling is for real. At one point, for example, Jane slaps Blanche. Going over that scene with a Moviola, stopping the action, running it back and watching it in slow motion half a dozen times, it doesn't look as if Bette pulled any punches. It looks as if she really let Crawford have it.

The film is an amazing study in what is commonly known today as S&M. The hammer murder of the maid, Elvira, is horrendous. The death scene on the beach, with Baby Jane and her strawberry ice cream cone performing to her audience as Blanche's life fades away might be one of the most remarkably subtle moments of horror ever recorded on film.

Bette did her own make-up, believing that Baby Jane was the kind of woman who instead of washing her face would simply lay on another coat of paint. *New Yorker* felt Bette had "rigged herself up as an elderly alcoholic harridan of unbearable frumpy ugliness." Aldrich used cuts from *Parachute Jumper* and *Ex-Lady* to show what a poor actress Jane Hudson had been while he took cuts out of Crawford's 1934 film *Sadie McKee* to prove that Blanche had been a star.

Of course, today *Baby Jane* is an "institution" among film buffs. Strangely enough in 1962 the reviews were mixed. It was obviously one of those films that needed to mature. Bette's performance earned her another Best Actress nomination, her tenth. Crawford's showing did not and that must have irked her no end. Bette lost to Anne Bancroft for *The Miracle Worker* and in a kind of grotesque one-upmanship straight out of *Baby Jane*, it was Joan Crawford who gloatingly accepted the Oscar for Anne Bancroft.

Nevertheless, Bette's success as Baby Jane Hudson started what so many newspapers called "A Davis Boom." In the *London Evening Standard*, under just such a headline, she was quoted as saying that until Baby Jane came along, "No picture of mine made a dime in the last ten years. The stories were so bad. And people decided I didn't draw the crowds any more. They didn't want me. I wasn't out of work. There were jobs I could do here or there. But I wanted to see if they were right. I thought why should thirty years of experience go down the drain? The result was *Baby Jane*, in the face of opposition from most top Hollywood people."

Whatever Happened To Baby Jane? *with Joan Crawford (inset right)* Parachute Jumper *with Douglas Fairbanks Jnr. and (left)* Ex-Lady *with Gene Raymond. Producer Robert Aldrich used cuts from these two films to prove what a bad actress Jane Hudson was.*

The Late Films

THE "DAVIS BOOM" WAS fast off the line but it took some doing before it moved into high gear. *The Lonely Life* sold well in hardback, went into serialization, then paperback. *Baby Jane* was packing them into the theatres and television wanted her for everything from guest appearances in weekly westerns to late night chat shows. But the moguls in Hollywood, the men who made movies, weren't quite as sure. Her memoires merely served to remind a lot of them how difficult she could be. Her frankness was astonishing but not everybody was pleased by it, or willing to slap her on the back for being honest. Okay, they agreed, *Baby Jane* was fine but it was a fluke. The ad. she ran in the trade papers in September 1962, merely a month after *Baby Jane* was previewed, confirmed their suspicions. In-work stars didn't advertise in the Situations Wanted columns. Obviously she didn't have lots of offers so she had to start begging. The moguls were more convinced than ever.

Except one.

And that one knew her very well.

Jack Warner hadn't dialled her number in more than a dozen years. They had seen each other on occasions over the years . . . *Baby Jane* was released by Warners but not shot there . . . anyway, that was Robert Aldrich's picture. Now Warner had one of his own. Thirty years after he first hired her, he wanted to hire her again. The film was to be called *Dead Ringer* . . . the British title was *Dead Image* . . . and her old chum Paul Henreid was to direct. At the same time Aldrich wanted her to do a special role in a Frank Sinatra-Dean Martin movie called *Four For Texas*. She accepted both but through a series of circumstances and changed dates on production schedules at Warners, she had to cancel out on her date with Aldrich. For the first time in more than a dozen years she drove back through the gates at Warners as a working star.

Co-starring Karl Malden, Peter Lawford, Philip Carey and Jean Hagen, Bette played twins for the second time in her career. Again using complicated split-screen techniques, she is first Edith Philips, a woman who owns a bar, then she is Edith's identical twin, Margaret De Lorca who has just lost her husband. Margaret wants to patch up their long-standing quarrel but Edith won't have it. Jealous of Margaret's wealth Edith lures her sister to her rather shabby flat, murders her and changes places with her. She writes a suicide note for herself then goes to live her sister's life. She manages to pull it off, until Margaret's lover Tony, played by Lawford, comes back from Europe and immediately knows something's amiss. The police sergeant investigating the case, played by Malden, happens to have been in love with Edith. He suspects that Margaret murdered her husband and sets out to prove it. In the end Edith as Margaret goes to jail. But to save her policeman from grieving that he is sending Edith to jail, she tells him Edith is dead and she is Margaret. Phew! Complicated stuff this one.

The critics didn't necessarily rave. *Time Magazine* said, "*Dead Ringer* is predicated on the proposition that two Bette Davis' are better than one". But then they felt, "Her acting, as always, isn't really acting. It's shameless showing off. But just try to look away." The *New York Times* found it an "uncommonly silly film," although they too added that it was "great fun to watch."

Her work with Henreid went smoothly. The two of them did what they could to bolster the script and because they worked well together they brought the film in several days ahead of schedule. Jack Warner must have been astonished.

Madame Sin.

Dead Ringer was also the last time that Bette worked with Ernest Haller. Often referred to as her favourite cameraman, he was born in 1896. After leaving school he worked briefly as a bank clerk before going into films in 1914 as an actor at the Biograph Studios. His in front-of-the-camera career was short lived, lasting less than twelve months and the following year he took a job in the studio's camera department. Between 1925 and 1951, he was one of the house-cameramen at First National/Warners, after which he freelanced around Hollywood and was generally regarded as one of the town's best. His credits include work on such classics as *The Dawn Patrol* directed by Howard Hawks, *Captain Blood* and *Mildred Pierce* for Michael Curtiz, and *Rebel Without A Cause.* He was often chosen as cameraman by directors such as Raoul Walsh, George Cukor and Frank Capra in addition to working with Bette on fourteen films, amongst them *Baby Jane, Dark Victory, Jezebel* and *Dangerous.* Only Perc Westmore and Orry-Kelly worked with her more often than Haller. The other cameramen who did a large number of films with her were Sol Polito with nine and Tony Gaudio with eleven. Haller won an Oscar for his photography of *Gone With The Wind.* He died in 1970.

Pleased to be working again, she went to Rome for Carlo Ponti who wanted her to play in *The Empty Canvas* with Horst Buchholz and Catherine Spaak. It was based on a story by Alberto Moravia called *Boredom.* And in the end there was no need to have changed the title. Ponti had promised Bette that the script would include additional scenes for her. When she got to Italy, nothing had been done to the script. She didn't get along very well with Buchholz, didn't speak Italian, couldn't understand why she had been hired in the first place and found the whole experience rather exasperating. The *New Yorker* called the film "one of the worst".

Released by Embassy Pictures, the boss there was Joseph E. Levine. He must have felt guilty that Bette had come out of it so displeased and perhaps to make it up to her, he offered her a part in his epic version of Harold Robbins' *Where Love Has Gone.* She was Mrs. Gerald Hayden, dowager mother of Valerie, played by Susan Hayward. Michael Connors was Luke Miller, Valerie's lover who is murdered by her daughter Danny, played by Joey Heatherton. It was all supposed to have been based on the true life story of Lana Turner and the killing of Johnny Stompanato.

Again, it did not turn out to be the kind of experience that Bette had hoped it might. She and Hayward didn't get along. She was constantly upset by Hayward's haughty behaviour and at one point she exploded on the set and threw a wig at Hayward. *Newsweek* thought the story was foolish but gave Bette ratings of "splendid, with her eyes rolling . . ." *Saturday Review* said she was "magnificent, bringing all her verve and intensity to the role . . ."

She left the set, thinking her work was over and teamed up again with Robert Aldrich for what might have been *Baby Jane-Two* but carried the title, *Hush . . . Hush, Sweet Charlotte.*

Then *Where Love Has Gone* came back to haunt her. Edward Dymtryk who directed and Levine who produced wanted Bette to do a new ending. They wanted Bette to show Mrs. Hayden going insane. Bette refused. They insisted that the ninety seconds of film they were asking for was necessary for the picture and that she was bound by contract to do it. Still Bette refused. They took her to court and slapped an injunction on her, preventing her from doing another film until this matter had been resolved. Bette's argument was simply that she had played a rational character throughout the film and that it would be inconsistent for such a woman to go insane in ninety seconds. The courts agreed with her.

Joan Crawford had been signed to co-star with Bette in *Hush . . . Hush, Sweet Charlotte* but she had to drop out due to illness. Production was held up for months waiting for Crawford who actually started the film then abandoned it. At Bette's suggestion her pal Olivia de Havilland was given the Crawford part of Miriam. Bette plays Charlotte Hollis, a Louisiana woman who refuses to give up her decrepit house just because a highway project is coming through her living room. That house had been the scene of her lover's beheading and in her mind the razing of the place would prove that her own father had murdered her lover. To prevent it she seeks help by inviting her cousin Miriam to visit. But instead of helping Miriam takes over, having plotted with Drew, the local physician, played by Joseph Cotton. The two know that Charlotte has money and they can get it by driving her insane. Miriam fires Charlotte's maid then murders her. She then convinces Charlotte to help her hide the body and says it is Drew. When they return to the house Charlotte sees Drew there and takes one more good-sized step off the deep end. But later she spots Drew and Miriam together on a balcony plotting against her and when she realizes what's been going on, she drops a cement pot on the two of them.

Perhaps because Bette and Olivia de Havilland personally got along so much better than Bette and Joan Crawford, the film lacks the edge that *Baby Jane* had. The cast was larger with Agnes Moorehead, Victor Buono, Mary Astor, Cecil Kellaway, George Kennedy and a young Bruce Dern and it was based more on the macabre than *Baby Jane* was. Maybe that's why the film wasn't called *Whatever Happened to Cousin Charlotte?* The point is that Aldrich was faced with a problem right from the start. He didn't seem to know if he should make another *Baby Jane* or something totally different. If *Hush . . . Hush, Sweet Charlotte* suffers from anything, that's probably it. *Time Magazine* must have felt the same way, because they said, "The two films are blood relatives, as Producer-Director Robert Aldrich well knows but *Charlotte* has a worse play, more gore, and enough bitchery to fill several outrageous freak shows." Yet all the critics agreed that once again Bette had turned in a splendid performance. "Choicest holdover from *Jane*," added *Time*, "is Bette Davis, unabashedly securing her clawhold as Hollywood's grande-dame ghoul." Arthur Knight, in the *Saturday Review* felt that Bette's performance immeasurably aided Aldrich's project. He said hers was a "Gutsy, free-wheeling performance," with her "incredible ability to abandon all consciousness of self in the full realization of a role that ranges from youthful, wide-eyed innocence to the stark terror of a middle-aged woman helplessly in the grip of a nightmare, both real and imagined".

Bette followed the film immediately by a series of personal appearances with Olivia de Havilland and at one point during the tour told the press, "No more macabre films for me".

But she didn't exactly keep her word because no one could confuse *The Nanny* with light comedy. Seven Arts and Hammer Films brought her to London in 1965 to star in a story about the problems between a nanny and a young boy. Produced and written by Jimmy Sangster, the film was directed by Seth Holt who had obviously been influenced by Hitchcock. Child star William Dix played Joey, Wendy Craig played his mother, with Bette ruling their lives. "I don't consider this a horror movie," she told the BBC. "You know, everybody acts in the press today as if anything that involves any kind of murder, legitimate or not, or any kind of tragedy is a horror movie."

This one certainly has its share of tragedy. Her neglect causes a child to drown in a bath tub. Joey knows his Nanny did it although everyone thinks him responsible. When his mother comes down with food poisoning, he is supposed to stay home alone with his Nanny but refuses. His aunt, played by Jill Bennett, comes to stay but is driven to her death. Joey says his Nanny is trying to drown him and she does, in fact, try. At the last minute, however, she stops, he escapes and she begins to pack. Her performance was thought to be nothing short of masterful. Some critics even compared her with George Arliss at the height of his maturity. Judith Christ, one of America's more perceptive reviewers wrote at the time, "Miss Davis is out for character rather than hoax and comes up with a beautifully controlled performance".

Alexander Walker, writing in *Stardom – The Hollywood Phenomenon* said that *The Nanny* held the character's real nature in suspension right to the end of the film, which meant that the audience never knew whether they were watching a tyrant who did what she did for everyone's good or merely for her own sadistic satisfaction. "She vibrated rather than acted, as if the actual striking of the precise note had taken place a split-second before the camera began shooting. Only a star like Davis could have sustained so well, or so long, the doubt about her real motives."

He had written about her, "The outer realism has always an inner logic," but when they met he found something he didn't seem to expect. He found a star in the truest sense of the word.

"It is prudent to stand still," he said about being in her presence, "as one is instructed on safari, and let her do the approaching. For Hollywood has bred in her a physical awareness of people, which is maybe why the memorable line in *All About Eve* . . . Fasten your seat belts, it's going to be a bumpy night . . . is uttered with a matchless sense of someone used to sniffing blood on the wind."

It might be that *The Nanny* was too British a film for the American audience. There's really no telling why it didn't score a hit in the United States. The fact is simply that it came and went quietly. When she returned home, she found enough television offers to keep her busy but it was still a problem to land great screen roles, mainly because there weren't any great parts for older women. There was talk she might play Martha in *Who's Afraid of Virginia Woolf?* but Elizabeth Taylor got the job. There was also talk she might play Maxine again, this time in the film version of *The Night Of The Iguana* but that part went to Ava Gardner. There was talk Aldrich would cast her in *The Killing Of Sister George* but in the end he chose Beryl Reid who had played it on stage. Then there was an offer from Paul Newman to work for one day as his mother in *Cool Hand Luke*. He reportedly offered her $25,000 for the day's shooting. But she turned it down supposedly because she wouldn't be on camera long enough to match the star billing that went with the offer and she worried that her fans might feel cheated. There was talk she might play Helen in *Valley of the Dolls* but that part went to Susan Hayward. There was talk she might play the title role in *The Greatest Mother Of Them All* but that film was shelved. So was *The Day The Plum Tree Shook* and her starring part in that.

She went back to London in 1968 at the invitation of Hammer Films again, to play Mrs. Taggart in *The Anniversary*, hoping that it might be as good a film as *The Nanny*. It wasn't.

Based on a play that ran in London's West End, Mrs. Taggart is a one-eyed shrew with three grown-up children and a flock of grandchildren who are subjected to her whims and fancies, including her wedding anniversary despite the fact that she has been widowed for ten years. The role is one of the great "monster-mothers" of all time. The film is a loser.

Bette wore an eye-patch throughout the film, making her fairly uncomfortable. On camera she hideously frightens her youngest son's fiancée by putting her glass eye where the girl will find it. She overly protects her oldest son whose main activity is stealing underwear off clothes lines. And she torments her middle son and his wife by bribing them with large amounts of money to do what she wants them to.

"It may not be the greatest movie ever made," she said, "but it's a good old fashioned Bette Davis movie and I do get the best of everybody in the end. And it was a challenge."

Challenge notwithstanding, it didn't seem to be a happy picture for her to do. She didn't get along with the original director and probably due to her, he was replaced. Some members of the cast had been in the stage version so it may have been a problem for her stepping into the middle of an already formed "group". Sheila Hancock was one of these, playing Bette's daughter-in-law who finally takes a stand against her mother-in-law. Now an established actress and stage director, Sheila says that when this film was made it was an impressive but not necessarily happy experience. "Bette Davis said to me early on, something like, 'I don't believe in happy films where everybody has a wonderful time on the set because those always turn out to be disasters at the box office.' And there's really no pretending. This was not a happy film."

It began before Bette's arrival with everyone making a lot of fuss about her. "But looking back," Sheila says, "I can see that the fuss was made about her, not by her. In fact, I never heard her demand anything. She probably found us as threatening as we

With William Campbell in Hush . . .
Hush, Sweet Charlotte.

found her."

Bette claims that following the director change, "The original stage cast fought me tooth and nail". But Sheila is sorry that Bette should have felt that way. "From her point of view, it must have been very difficult stepping into a film to work with people who had been a team on stage together. I can see where she felt upset about that and it was unfortunate for her to be in that position. I heard years later that she thought of us as being stand-offish. I guess in a way we were but it was mostly out of awe. We thought that's what she wanted. I regret it now and quite frankly wish I had somehow been able to get up my nerve and invite her back to the flat for a meal. I think she would have liked that."

Putting personal differences aside, Sheila says that on the set Bette was the epitome of professionalism. "Despite her star reputation, she was quite the opposite. At the end of the day, for example, even though she was tired, she'd do our close-ups with us. She wouldn't just read out lines, she'd actually stand off camera giving us our lines with a whole performance."

It seems Bette's years of experience showed. "They showed in everything she did," Sheila continues, "She knew her lines right from the start. She was deadletter perfect. She knew how she wanted her make-up, and she knew lighting so well that she knew how she could best be lit for her scenes. Her dedication and her talent for knowing what she could make work was immensely impressive. I had never met such a total and utter professional."

The reviews were fairly dismal and rightfully so. Yet there are a few moments in the film that show her power. She makes an entrance at the very beginning that is worthy of Elizabeth I. When she's given a *mannequin pis* toy as a present, she pulls the string, watches the little boy do his trick, and cackles with such wonderful vulgarity that you'd think she was actually having a good time.

She did nothing else until she returned to England a year later for a film with Michael Redgrave, *Connecting Rooms*. She had seen the script a couple of years earlier and liked the idea that it had nothing to do with horror or murder or blood. It's the story of a fifty-one year old cellist, played by Bette, who lives in a rooming house with Redgrave playing a homosexual and Alexis Kanner as a pop-singer. Franklin Gollings directed his own screenplay. "It was a complete change of pace for me," Bette told the *Los Angeles Herald-Examiner*. A pleasant bit of trivia about this film is that, for the cello-playing scenes, Bette's hands were tied behind her back with other arms playing the music. Those other arms belonged to Amorlis Fleming, sister of James Bond's creator, Ian. *Connecting Rooms* was not released in England for some two years and, except for very limited showings in the United States, it did nothing. No one could find much to praise about the film and even the British Film Institute's Monthly Film Bulletin, which is usually much less severe than lots of critics, wrote that it was a "Doomed attempt to locate an old-fashioned, melodramatic romance in a contrived, contemporary setting."

She did another television guest shot, this time with Robert Wagner in his series *It Takes A Thief*. Bette had worked with Wagner's late wife, Natalie Wood and the two got along so well that a few years later Wagner produced a made-for-television movie called *Madame Sin*. They also posed together for a whiskey advertisement. That ad. was a lot more successful than *Madame Sin*. Wagner had hoped it could be made into a series. No one in any of the television networks agreed with him.

In 1971, a film company called American International Pictures decided it might be a good idea to rematch Bette with Ernest Borgnine and they came up with *Bunny O'Hare*. Originally called *Bunny and Billy*, she played the part of a grandmother who, with her ex-thief boyfriend goes into the bank robbing business, à la Robin Hood. Dressed as hippies, they race around Albuquerque, New Mexico on a motorcycle. It was the first time Bette had ever done an "all location" motion picture. And her discomfort while doing the film meant that it would also be her last. She told interviewers at the time that she couldn't think of any reason why a film had to be made on location like this when everything would be much easier and the actors much more comfortable working on the back of a Hollywood lot.

That wasn't the only problem with this film. In the beginning she went on record saying, "It's an intelligent script, it's funny, there's lots in it that's sweet and nice, and it has a lot to say in it's mild little way." But once it was finished, she sued the production company for a reported $5 million, charging them with fraudulant misrepresentation because the version of the film to be distributed to theatres across the country was "tastelessly and inarticulately assembled." Even the director, Gerd Oswald testified on her behalf, claiming the picture had been mutilated after he turned in his final cut. "They made a different film from that which we had conceived." Some of the critics thought she was very funny, such as Vincent Canby of the *New York Times.* Others agreed with her that the film was awful.

While it was being shot, she took time off to go to Boston where she presented the Boston University Library with her collection of film and theatre books, with scripts, "with all of my records of whatever I have accomplished". On that trip, she talked with Nora Taylor of the *Christian Science Monitor.* "It is my aim," Bette said, "to die with my name above the title. But to do this means a constant search for suitable scripts. If you have a desire not to be a supporting player you have trouble finding scripts. They are hard to come by for an older person like me."

Taylor asked if movie-making in the '70s was different from the way it was when Bette first started and the answer was, "It's not as professional now. It's short cut, and really a retrogression. Films are being done now with the short cuts that were being used in 1930 before they went on to some important films."

Bunny O'Hare didn't go very far and Bette moved on to her next project. She signed with British actress Anne Heywood to play in *And Presumed Dead,* a thriller about kidnapping that she felt held promise but the movie was never made because the producers couldn't raise the money. Times had certainly changed.

Madame Sin's appearance on television was followed by another made for TV film called *The Judge and Jake Wyler.* In the former she played an Oriental villainess. In the latter she portrayed a hypochrondiac judge who owns a detective agency and employs a couple of ex-convicts. Again it was to be a series pilot but no one picked it up. Universal Pictures added a few scenes and turned it into a two-hour TV special.

She followed that by going to Rome to film *Lo Scopone Scientifico* but it turned out to be almost as big a fiasco as *The Empty Canvas* had been. The English titles were *The Scientific Cardplayer* and *The Game* a film described in a press handout as "A true story about a famous card game, which is more a game of strength. One plays on the rebound, in other words, each sum temporarily won must be replaced on the card table for the next round, the best do not win, the winners are those that can prolong the game until infinity. The one who wins commands and whoever commands continues to win the stakes of the game, that is the money. Here the winning hero is the money."

Right away you can see what she was up against. On top of that, the film was to be made in Italian although everyone on the set spoke English. Alberto Sordi, for instance, whose English is perfect, refused to speak to Bette except in Italian. The director, Luigi Comencini provided her with an interpreter so that he could bark at her in Italian and she would have to wait for the translation before being able to answer. Understandably, the movie has never gone down as one of America's most memorable screen creations. Or even Italy's.

Again she made a stab at a weekly TV series. This one was called *Hello Mother, Goodbye* but nothing came of it. She went from that to a film for television called *Scream Pretty Peggy* . . . an NBC Movie of the Week. She played the psychopathic murderer's alcoholic mother. In 1974, still thinking that the stage might hold greater promise she signed to star as Miss Moffat in the Joshua Logan musical version of *The Corn Is Green.* Emlyn Williams and Logan had updated the storyline, added original music and hoped they were riding a winner. When it tried out in Philadelphia in October 1974 the reviews weren't good. Before the month was out the play closed. Bette had suffered a recurrence of her back injury and couldn't work. Logan and

Williams decided not to replace her. They folded their tent and she eventually went on the road with her own one-woman show. Film clips, a talk, answering question from the audience . . . she was such a hit across the country, especially with University audiences that she took herself to Australia and England where she was a resounding success. It all helped to rebuild her confidence, so that in 1975 when Dan Curtis told her he was producing and directing a thriller she said she might be interested. He said he wanted her to play Oliver Reed's aunt in *Burnt Offerings* but she said she wouldn't do it if, "I disappear in a sneeze." Curtis said that wouldn't happen. But her role was small and she didn't get along with Oliver Reed at all. The reviews were lousy and, despite her very minor role, in some theatres she was deceptively billed as the star.

Willing to keep at it and try something new, in 1976 she recorded an album with the London based EMI Records called *Miss Bette Davis*. You can't say she actually sings. It's more talk-singing. But she does some of her "earlier hits" such as *They're Either Too Young Or Too Old* and *I've Written A Letter To Daddy*. She also does a speech from *All About Eve*, plus a dramatic rendition of *Mother Of The Bride*. She might not have made the charts but it's a camp record that is actually kind of neat. She's certainly no Fred Astaire, but then again, Fred Astaire is no Bette Davis.

She did a few more television specials. In *The Disappearance of Aimé* she was cast as Faye Dunaway's mother with the two of them being billed above the title . . . and her reviews were characteristically good. She followed that with *The Dark Secret Of Harvest Home*, then the highly acclaimed *Strangers – The Story Of A Mother And Daughter* for which she won an Emmy, and then *Skyward* under Ron Howard's direction. In between there were guest shots, talk shows and, of course, the American Film Institute tribute. But feature films were few and far between.

In 1978 she did a cameo in *Death On The Nile*, the Agatha Christie story directed by John Guillermin with a cast of stars such as Peter Ustinov, David Niven, Mia Farrow, Angela Lansbury and Maggie Smith. Bette's role was small, almost too small, as Mrs. Van Schuyler, one of the passengers on the river cruise. Maggie Smith played Bowers, her personal secretary. And while the film is filled with the usual who dunnit twists, there is a brief few seconds of wonderfully pure Bette Davis. Bowers complains about a trip ashore by telling Mrs. Van Schuyler, "If there are two things I can't stand, it's heat and natives." And Bette gives her a marvellous look and with all her panache announces, "Then we'll go."

That same year she signed up with Walt Disney to do what might well have been her first kids' picture. *Return From Witch Mountain* co-starred Christopher Lee as the scientist who can turn humans into robots. Bette as Letha Wedge is the woman who finances his research. The film was directed by John Hough who also directed her next effort, called *The Watcher In The Woods*, also for Disney. There she co-stars with David McCallum and Carroll Baker. She plays Mrs. Aylwood, a woman who lives in the middle of a forest, never having forgotten the eerie disappearance of her daughter thirty years ago.

She seems slightly uncomfortable at times in *Return From Witch Mountain* and *The Watcher In The Woods* will never be considered classic Disney. But there are moments in both films where you know that fifty years of experience are behind every word. In *Return From Witch Mountain* for example, the kids have won and Bette and Christopher Lee are trapped at the top of a scaffolding in the middle of a huge factory boiler room. The end has come for the villains and all Bette can do is look down at them and mumble aside, "It's shocking how they raise kids these days."

The Nanny.

The Last Chapter

"WHAT SHALL I CALL YOU?" he asked the first day they met.

"A few years ago it would have been Miss Davis," she said. "Now, well, call me Bette."

Return To Witch Mountain was John Hough's eighth film. It was Bette's eighty-fourth, not counting all the films she made for television. He had worked previously with stars but never anyone as legendary as Bette. "She was tough when she had to be tough," he says, "but she always knew what she was doing. At one point during *Return To Witch Mountain* there was a comment made about the dress she'd wear in the last scene. Bette and I decided she'd be in black. But the wardrobe people came by and said that because the scene would be shot with her on a scaffold in the darkened corner of a boiler room, she should be wearing something light so she could be seen. Bette glared at them and said, 'I've made eighty films and sixty of them were in black and white. In fifty of those I wore black clothes. If you can't see me up there this time, fire the cameraman.'"

Another side of Bette came to light with that scaffold scene when John Hough found out she was afraid of heights. "She asked if a double could go up. I said no. She said she just couldn't do it because she was terrified of heights. The next morning at about three she woke me up to tell me that if I really wanted her to she would. She's that much of a professional!"

So much a professional, he says that it shows clearly in everything she does. "We were pressed for time at one point and I told the crew to hurry along so that we could get a quick close up of Miss Davis. She overheard me and announced, 'There is no such thing as a quick close up of Miss Davis.'"

For another scene, Hough was talking to an actor about his motivation for a scene, with Bette standing near by. Hough was explaining how he wanted the actor to react when the actor, whom Hough won't name, cut in with, "But I wouldn't want to take anything away from Miss Davis." At that moment Bette snapped, "Do your damnedest, because Miss Davis can take care of herself."

Hough found out early just how Bette can and does take care of herself. He called her for eight o'clock on the first morning of *Return To Witch Mountain*. When it was time, he and the crew were still standing around, setting up the shots, drinking coffee, making ready for the day's work. He looked up and saw Bette standing on her mark, in costume and make-up. She was ready to go. "It taught everyone a lesson," he says. "When you call her, she's there and she expects you to be ready for her. The only thing she demands is that everybody is as professional as she. In both films I made with her I never heard her demand anything else. I found that when she wasn't in a scene she'd be sitting on the set. It frightened some of the others because they all thought she was judging them, but that wasn't it at all. She'd sit there trying to see how she could improve her work by better understanding the story."

He says she never permits anything to get in the way of her work, not even her ego. She is totally honest with herself. In *Watcher In The Woods* there's a flashback scene where Mrs. Aylwood is shown as a young woman, forty years earlier. Bette wanted to play that part too but Hough had reservations. She asked that before he cast anyone else, she be tested. They did wardrobe and make-up and he says the transformation was staggering but he couldn't convince himself that it would be right. He worried about how he was going to tell her that it didn't work and after they looked at the rushes, the two of them were left alone to discuss it. "I knew she couldn't span the age gap," Hough recounts, "but telling her that is a

As Mrs. Van Schuyler in Death On The Nile

moment every director would have to dread. I sat there for a moment trying to decide how to say it. She asked me what I thought. I finally told her I didn't think it could work. Suddenly she burst out laughing, 'You're Goddamned right it won't.' ''

"She's such a perfectionist," he continues. "In every way. The day she arrives on the set she knows the whole script. She never fluffs a line, she's letter perfect and never makes a mistake. She wants her make-up, wardrobe and hair perfect and when it's not she's very, very tough. But it's such a pleasure to work with someone like that. To see all those years of experience come in to play."

All those years of experience have taught her the tricks of her trade and Hough says even the veterans on the set were impressed. For instance, just before the camera rolls, she always looks down so when the director shouts "Action" she can bring her eyes up and they're filled with life. She likes to know where her key-light is to make sure she is being well photographed, then before every take she'd always lick her lips. If I sound star-struck when I talk about working with her, well, you have to understand that everbody is. Come on, just look at who we're talking about. I mean, how can anybody not be star-struck with Bette Davis?"

The great *New Yorker Magazine* writer Janet Flanner certainly was nearly forty years ago when she wrote a major article called *Cotton-Dress Girl: Bette Davis.* "Miss Davis' success has been constructed on her tendency not to be recognized," she wrote in her opening paragraph. "She arrived in Hollywood with nothing positive but her intelligence, and that was against her. Negatively, Hollywood said her smile was crooked, her cranium the wrong shape, her mouth too small, her eyes too large, her neck too long, and her erotic appeal devoid of any dimensions whatever. Furthermore, her figure was mandolin rather than guitar. Universal Studios, which had the misfortune to hold her first contract and not renew it, thought her a tense young woman who would never get anywhere. There Carl Laemmle Jr. dismissed her as 'a cotton dress girl', satin sweethearts then being, sociologically speaking, box-office."

Few writers have ever summed it up better but then Janet Flanner was one of those writers whose insights transferred well on to paper. And her insights about Bette seem very much on target, even all these years later. "In her Hollywood history she has fought her way from the bottom to the top and more than once part way back again. She is a militant, lively New England character with portable principles, which she has enjoyed scrapping for on Western studio soil."

Flanner goes on with adjectives such as, "Disciplined but unpredictable," and also "mettlesome". Then she says that Bette "Is an individualist, and Hollywood, which once coarsely summed up this quality as a headache, now with much refinement calls her forthright. Anyone who tries to drive her gets into trouble, though she can usually be led." She also makes a point of noting, "Her almost regal power in Hollywood still startles her."

To research the article, Flanner spoke with some of Bette's directors, although she doesn't name them, preferring simply to explain, "Her directors say that for Davis to get going at her best she needs to play an intelligent female who is either wrong or wronged, a cerebral skirt, preferably with black conscience and somehow entangled with fate, against a background of earthquake, upper-class murder, or historical crisis."

It seems that some directors confided in Flanner that Bette was interesting to work with and that no other actress of the day was as interesting, "Once the preliminary discussion of what is to be done has died down". They said she was also an actress of great integrity. "She won't even cross to the coffee table, centre-left, unless she has a conviction about it. Her disagreements with directors usually arise from the fact that she is still more theatre-minded than movie-minded."

Pointing out that Bette habitually favours stage realism over tricks for the camera, Flanner cites Bette's insistence during *Watch On The Rhine* on wearing cotton stockings instead of silk which would have photographed better. Cotton was what her character would have worn, so cotton it was. The same kind of problem arose when Bette made *Bordertown*. That was the incident where she was to be shown getting out of bed in the morning, and so she smeared her face with cold cream and messed up her hair, only to wind up arguing with the director who thought she looked like she was just getting out of bed. Yet Flanner found that those directors, "Mostly agree that her psychological diagnosis of a role can stabilize a whole picture, that she never throws a good line away, that her talent and technique never dry up, which in movie making means that the final take, which may be the fiftieth repetition, done at sundown, is as fresh and careful as the first, done after breakfast."

At the time Flanner wrote about Bette, in 1943, she had done fifty-two pictures. The article says Bette's contract called for her to work forty weeks a year and be paid $5,500 a week. With radio work bringing in another $50,000 a year, Flanner guessed that Bette would be making somewhere near a quarter of a million dollars a year.

"Becoming a star often addles a human being," Flanner continued, suggesting that it happens in one of only three ways. Either that person becomes a superior, lonely ego and stays home, a public figure, often seen in public or finally, glamorous no matter where he or she happens to be. "Miss Davis was glamorous, years ago for about a month. This period ended when, backed up by a smart town-car containing a white poodle and liveried chauffeur, and attired in moody black velvet slacks and jacket, she met her mother, who had been on a trip back east, at the Los Angeles railway station. Mrs. Davis was unable to believe her own eyes and flatly said so. The glamour was dropped later that day."

What Flanner found instead of a glamour girl, was a woman who closely resembled her screen roles. A woman who was vital, arresting, restless and informal. "She gestures a great deal, as in *The Little Foxes,* and has a nervous tic of tossing her head, as in *The Old Maid.* She also has a woodwind laugh. Her conversation is pertinent, stimulating and personal. It is animated by sudden ideas, reactions, and asides, almost as if she were talking to herself, which as a matter of fact she says she does, and those serve for her as temporary conclusions. Her vocabulary is a mixture of slang and polysyllables. It used to be rather like a Restoration comedy until some cameraman made a film of one of her heated studio arguments. As she watched the picture, she remarked, 'My damns seem monotonous,' and started breaking the habit. She still smokes a lot, that always having been her second vice."

Some people have referred to Bette as one of only two stars in Hollywood who has ever known how to smoke, the other being Bogart. Smoking on screen is one of the mannerisms that seems to be her, like that certain way she snaps her eyelids shut. It's the stuff that screen trademarks are made out of. She herself isn't sure however, and in *Films and Filming Magazine* she was once quoted as saying, "One of the things over the years that critics have repeatedly referred to have been my mannerisms. Well, it depends what part I'm playing. I can show you just as many parts where I didn't flutter one eyelid, ever."

At the same time, Bette did an interview with the BBC in London but instead of talking about her acting technique, they asked her which films she liked the most. "Among my films," she answered, "I always put *Dark Victory* first. I certainly add *All About Eve.* I certainly enjoyed *Jezebel.* I certainly enjoyed making *Juarez.* And another film that was never heard of at all in America because it was such a flop and was treated much more kindly in Britain was *Wedding Breakfast* (The US title was *The Catered Affair*) one of the favourite parts I ever played. I always say about that one, when I die may be they'll re-release it in America and they will have some kind of respect."

Strangely enough she didn't include *Baby Jane* which she had made only a few years before that interview. But then when you've made as many films as she has, it's not easy picking only a few as favourites. About fifteen years later she was asked the same question by a British journalist who got this as an answer: "Favourite films? There were lots. *Dark Victory. Jezebel. Now, Voyager. Whatever Happened to Baby Jane?* Why *Jane?* Because it was a great part and making it was so much fun. Oh yes, I liked it much more than *Hush . . . Hush, Sweet Charlotte.* The one film I hated was *Burnt Offerings.* It was a hideous mess."

Strangely enough, this time she didn't mention *All About Eve*.

Actually it must be somewhat confusing for anyone who's done so much work to remember every bit of it, or even most of it. Then again, the film that gets released to the theatres is not necessarily the film as she would remember it. For her it would be a month or two of work, of people, of takes and retakes and of solving problems. The hundred or so minutes of celluloid that emerges is only a small part. Surrounding the entire project has also been her fight for survival. "What it takes to survive in Hollywood?" She told the London *Evening Standard* back in the late '60s, "Well, number one is the strength of an ox. Number two, a short memory of who did what to you."

If a short memory is part of the survival kit for Hollywood, it wasn't the case with Broadway. "I hate the theatre and never intend to do it again," she said to the *Hollywood Reporter* in 1973. "I hate the hours and the life. And half the New York audiences are not worth your time any more."

Yet one of the things that everyone seemed to have noticed about her, at least in the very early days, was her theatre background. Critics have always referred to her as an actress, not a movie-star. Way back in 1939 she wrote an article for *The Christian Science Monitor* where she told the world that her stage experience merely "gave me confidence to face the terrifying ordeal of early screen tests and those first trials before camera and microphones in regular production." The techniques, she said, for stage and film were too different to do anything more. "If the media weren't widely different, people who were so well adapted to one wouldn't fail in the other. On the other hand, those who have attained conspicuous success on both stage and screen have undoubtedly been qualified to cope successfullly with the problems of both media. They're double-threat artists. Whether or not I might have been in their class, I can't say. I was tremendously fond of the stage and would have been driven hard by my ambition. Critics said some nice things about my work in *Broken Dishes* and *Solid South*. I feel that I'd have succeeded. But what I think and feel doesn't prove anything. The fact remains that I came into pictures before I had reached any notable stature on the stage, and there was no telling what was actually in store for me behind the footlights, fame or flop."

Totally honest with herself right from the beginning, she never seemed to lose sight of the fact that she could have flopped in either medium.

These days her honesty is still evident. "I've no thoughts about retirement," she told Iain McAsh in *Stage And Screen Magazine*, showing that the drive is still there. "I work to keep alive. I love it. Besides, what else could I do?" And then to prove that nothing's changed, she added, "I am adamant that my name remains above the title. I fought for that. In films today, everyone's a star. They're billed as 'starring' or 'also starring'. In my day we earned it." Funny, but when he asked her if she'd seen all her movies, she told him flatly no. "I haven't seen all the old movies I've been in but I watch some of them again on television. They're on all the time in the States. And some of them are better than I thought." In those days she addmitted, "I couldn't bear my face. I got so depressed I couldn't watch the rushes." Now she says she sees herself and wonders, " 'What are you beefing about? You look absolutely gorgeous.' Those old Hollywood cameramen were masters."

Of course it wasn't just the cameramen, any more than it is just the cameramen who make stars today. Yes, times have changed, but she told McAsh that some things still remain. "When choosing scripts I always look for a good story first. Then who's going to be in it and directing. I always have co-star approval now. That's something I fought for. Of today's actresses I admire Barbra Streisand, Glenda Jackson and Jane Fonda. Women had the town (Hollywood) for twenty years. George Brent used to say all the men needed was a good haircut at the back. They only showed the back of their heads. And today's men? Well, the supermen are Redford, Newman and the admirable Mr. Peck. Roger Moore is a great guy. Errol Flynn was a naughty boy, but he had great charm and personality. British stars? I have a passion for Alan Bates. He's always excellent."

Family Reunion, *Miss Davis' latest made-for-television October, 1981.*

As for television, she said in that interview that she saw no difference between making television today or a movie. "TV crews work fast but don't forget we made *Jezebel* in six weeks." Yet some things have not necessarily changed for the better. "In those days," she went on, "you made seven or eight films a year. I made fourteen films in two years. It was non-stop work. Parts were written for you, roles to suit your personality. We never went outside Warner Studios, not even for big scenes. We had the same group, the same cameraman, hairdressers, make-up, assistant directors. We knew each other, perhaps because we saw more of each other than our own families. I feel sorry for crews today. They work on locations so much they're hardly ever at home to see their families." Locations, it turns out, are among her least favourite things. "Locations are all tough and they're all miserable. I never left the sound stage for eighteen years. We built a Welsh village, the petrified forest and the palace for Carlotta."

McAsh's story about Bette was published in October 1979, and almost ironically, it ran right next to a small blurb announcing the death in Hollywood of Carl Laemmle, Jr. The last paragraph of his obituary notes, "In his day, 'Junior' was a very powerful studio executive. He will always be remembered, however, as the man who, on viewing newcomer Bette Davis in Universal's *Bad Sister,* exclaimed, 'Wow! She has about as much sex appeal as Slim Summerville.'"

Three newspaper columns away, Bette remaked to McAsh, "I arrived in Hollywood in 1930, around Christmas. Universal signed me, then I was fired by Carl Laemmle, Jr. as being 'hopeless'."

Exactly half a century later and half a page away, Laemmle Jr. seems to have been very wrong.

THE MALL AT WINFIELD

Filmography - Theatre - T.V.

NOTE:
THIS IS A COMPLETE list of all the films of Bette Davis, including names of producers, directors and various other people involved in each film. The cast listed includes only the principal players in each film or, as in the case of earlier films, bit players who eventually became stars. Running times as listed are only approximate as some of the earlier films no longer exist and in some cases notes on their running times vary by a few minutes. Finally, the symbol * denotes a film that marks an important step in Bette Davis' career. These particular films are therefore something of a cross section of the best of her work, and serious Bette Davis fans should see them all.

1 *BAD SISTER* – Universal 1931. 68 minutes. Producer – Carl Laemmle, Jr. Director – Hobart Henley. Based on *The Flirt* by Booth Tarkington. Cast: Conrad Nagel, Sydney Fox, Bette Davis, Zasu Pitts, Slim Summerville and Humphrey Bogart.

2 *SEED* – Universal 1931. 96 minutes. Produced and directed by John Stahl. Cast: John Boles, Genevieve Tobin, Lois Wilson, Raymond Hackett, Bette Davis and Zasu Pitts.

3 *WATERLOO BRIDGE* – Universal 1931. 72 minutes. Producer – Carl Laemmle, Jr. Director – James Whale. Based on a play by Robert Sherwood. Cast: Mae Clarke, Kent Douglass (later to be called Douglass Montgomery), Doris Lloyd, Ethel Griffies, Bette Davis and Enid Bennett.

4 *WAY BACK HOME* – RKO 1932. 81 minutes. Producer – Pandro S. Berman. Director – William Seiter. Based on characters from the radio programmes of Phillips H. Lord. The original screenplay title was *Other People's Business*. Cast: Phillips Lord, Effie Palmer, Mrs. Phillips Lord, Frank Albertson and Bette Davis.

5 *THE MENACE* – Columbia 1932. 64 minutes. Producer – Sam Nelson. Director – Roy William Neil. Based on the Edgar Wallace book *The Featherbed Serpent*. Cast: H. B. Warner, Bette Davis, Walter Byron, Natalie Moorehead and Murray Kinnell.

6 *HELL'S HOUSE* – Capital Films Exchange 1932. 72 minutes. Producer – Benjamin F. Zeidman. Director – Howard Higgin. Cast: Junior Dirkin, Pat O'Brien, Bette Davis, Junior Coghlan, Charlie Grapewin and Emma Dunn.

7* *THE MAN WHO PLAYED GOD* – Warner Brothers 1932. 80 minutes. Producer – Jack Warner. Director – John Adolphi. Costumes – Orry-Kelly. Make-up – Perc Westmore. Cast: George Arliss, Violet Heming, Ivan Simpson, Louise Closser Hale, Bette Davis, Donald Cook, Ray Milland, Murray Kinnell and Hedda Hopper.

8 *SO BIG* – Warner Brothers 1932. 80 minutes. Producer – Jack Warner. Director – William Wellman. Based on the novel by Edna Ferber. Costumes – Orry-Kelly. Cast: Barbara Stanwyck, George Brent, Dickie Moore, Guy Kibbee, Bette Davis, Mae Madison, Hardie Albright, Alan Hale, Dawn O'Day, Dick Winslow and Dorothy Peterson.

9* *THE RICH ARE ALWAYS WITH US* – First National in association with Warner Brothers 1932. 73 minutes. In charge of production – Darryl Zanuck. Director – Alfred E. Green. Costumes – Orry-Kelly. Photography – Ernest Haller. Cast: Ruth Chatterton, George Brent, Adrienne Dore, Bette Davis, Robert Warwick, Eula Guy and Mae Madison.

10 *THE DARK HORSE* – First National with Warner Brothers 1932. 75 minutes. In charge of production – Darryl Zanuck. Director – Alfred E. Green. Based on an original story of Darryl Zanuck under the byline Melville Crossman. Cast: Warren William, Bette Davis, Guy Kibbee, Frank McHugh, Vivienne Osborne, Sam Hardy and Robert Warwick.

11* *CABIN IN THE COTTON* – First National with Warner Brothers 1932. 79 minutes. Producer Jack Warner. Director – Michael Curtiz. Bette made her singing debut in this film, doing a rendition of "Willie The Weeper". Cast: Richard Barthelmess, Dorothy Jordan, Bette Davis, Hardie Albright, Dorothy Peterson and Snowflake Toones.

12 *THREE ON A MATCH* – First National with Warner Brothers 1932. 63 minutes. In charge of production – Darryl Zanuck. Director – Mervyn Leroy. Cast: Joan Blondell, Warren William, Ann Dvorak, Bette Davis, Grant Mitchell, Lyle Talbot, Glenda Farrell and Humphrey Bogart.

13 *20,000 YEARS IN SING SING* – First National with Warner Brothers 1932. 77 minutes. In charge of production – Darryl Zanuck. Director – Michael Curtiz. Costumes – Orry-Kelly. This is the only film Bette ever did with Spencer Tracy. Cast: Spencer Tracy, Bette Davis, Lyle Talbot, Sheila Terry and Louis Calhern.

14 *PARACHUTE JUMPER* – Warner Brothers 1933. 65 minutes. Producer – Jack Warner. Director – Alfred E. Green. Cast: Douglas Fairbanks, Jr., Leo Carrillo, Bette Davis, Frank McHugh and Claire Dodd.

15 *THE WORKING MAN* – Warner Brothers/Vitaphone 1933. 73 minutes. In charge of production – Darryl Zanuck. Director – John Adolfi. Costumes – Orry-Kelly. Cast: George Arliss, Bette Davis, Hardie Albright, Theodore Newton, Gordon Westcott and J. Farrell MacDonald.

16 *EX-LADY* – Warner Brothers/Vitaphone 1933. 62 minutes. In charge of production – Darryl Zanuck. Director – Robert Florey. Costumes Orry-Kelly. Cast: Bette Davis, Gene Raymond, Frank McHugh and Claire Dodd.

17 *BUREAU OF MISSING PERSONS* – First National with Warner Brothers 1933. 75 minutes. Producer – Henry Blanke. Director – Roy Del Ruth. Cast: Bette Davis, Lewis Stone, Pat O'Brien, Glenda Farrell, Allen Jenkins, Ruth Donnelly and Alan Dinehart.

18 *FASHIONS OF 1934* – First National with Warner Brothers 1933. 77 minutes. Producer – Henry Blanke. Director – William Dieterle. Dances staged by Busby Berkeley. Costumes – Orry-Kelly. Cast: William Powell, Bette Davis, Frank McHugh, Verree Teasdale, Reginald Owen, Hobart Cavanaugh and Arthur Treacher.

19 *THE BIG SHAKEDOWN* – First National with Warner Brothers 1934. 64 minutes. Producer – Sam Bischoff. Director – John Francis Dillon. Cast: Charles Farrell, Bette Davis, Ricardo Cortez, Glenda Farrell, Allen Jenkins, Henry O'Neill and George Pat Collins.

20 *JIMMY THE GENT* – Warner Brothers/Vitaphone 1934. 66 minutes. Producer – Jack Warner. Director – Michael Curtiz. Cast: James Cagney, Bette Davis, Alice White, Allen Jenkins, Alan Dinehart, Mayo Methot, Hobart Cavanaugh and Dennis O'Keefe.

21 *FOG OVER FRISCO* – First National with Warner Brothers 1934. 67 minutes. Producer – Robert Lord. Director – William Dieterle. Cast: Bette Davis, Donald Woods, Margaret Lindsay, Lyle Talbot, Arthur Byron, Alan Hale and William Demarest.

22* *OF HUMAN BONDAGE* – RKO 1934. 83 minutes. Producer – Pandro S. Berman. Director – John Cromwell. Based on the novel by Somerset Maugham. Music – Max Steiner. Cast: Leslie Howard, Bette Davis, Frances Dee, Reginald Owen, Reginald Denny, Kay Johnson, Alan Hale, Reginald Sheffield and Desmond Roberts.

23 *HOUSEWIFE* – Warner Brothers/Vitaphone 1934. 69 minutes. Producer – Jack Warner. Director – Alfred E. Green. Costumes – Orry-Kelly. Cast: George Brent, Ann Dvorak, Bette Davis, John Halliday, Robert Barrat, Hobart Cavanaugh, Ruth Donnelly, Eula Guy and Leila Bennett.

24* *BORDERTOWN* – Warner Brothers/Vitaphone 1934. 69 minutes. Producer – Jack Warner. Director – Archie Mayo. Cast: Paul Muni, Bette Davis, Margaret Lindsay, Gavin Gordon, Arthur Stone, Robert Barrat, Soledad Jiminez, William B. Davidson, Hobart Cavanaugh, Henry O'Neill, Addie McPhail and Oscar Apfel.

25 *THE GIRL FROM TENTH AVENUE* – First National with Warner Brothers 1935. 69 minutes. Producer – Robert Lord. Director – Alfred E. Green. Costumes – Orry-Kelly. Cast: Bette Davis, Ian Hunter, Colin Clive, Alison Skipworth, John Eldredge, Phillip Reed, Katherine Alexander and Helen Jerome Eddy.

26 *FRONT PAGE WOMAN* – Warner Brothers/Vitaphone 1935. 80 minutes. Producer – Samuel Bischoff. Director – Michael Curtiz. Cast: Bette Davis, George Brent, Roscoe Karns, Winifred Shaw, June Martel, Dorothy Dare, J. Carroll Naish and DeWitt Jennings.

27 *SPECIAL AGENT* – Claridge Pictures with Warner Brothers 1935. 76 minutes. Producer – Samuel Bischoff in association with Martin Mooney. Director – William Keighley. Cast: Bette Davis, George Brent, Ricardo Cortez, Joseph Sawyer, Joseph Crehan, Henry O'Neill, J. Carroll Naish, Paul Guilfoyle and Robert Barrat.

28* *DANGEROUS* – Warner Brothers/Vitaphone 1935. 78 minutes. Producer – Harry Joe Brown. Director – Alfred E. Green. Costumes – Orry-Kelly. Photography – Ernest Haller. This was the film that won Bette her first Academy Award for Best Actress. Cast: Bette Davis, Franchot Tone, Margaret Lindsay, Alison Skipworth, John Eldredge, Dick Foran and William Davidson.

29 *THE PETRIFIED FOREST* – Warner Brothers/Vitaphone 1936. 75 minutes. Producer – Henry Blanke. Director – Archie Mayo. Based on a novel by Robert Sherwood. Costumes – Orry-Kelly. Cast: Leslie Howard, Bette Davis, Genevieve Tobin, Dick Foran, Humphrey Bogart, Joe Sawyer, Nina Campana, Charley Grapewin and Eddie Acuff.

30 *THE GOLDEN ARROW* – First National with Warner Brothers 1936. 68 minutes. Producer – Samuel Bischoff. Director – Alfred E. Green. Costumes – Orry-Kelly. Cast: Bette Davis, George Brent, Carol Hughes, Eugene Pallette, Dick Foran, Catherine Doucet, Hobart Cavanaugh, Henry O'Neill, Craig Reynolds, Eddie Acuff and Earl Foxe.

31 *SATAN MET A LADY* – Warner Brothers/Vitaphone 1936. 66 minutes. Producer – Henry Blanke. Director – William Dieterle. Costumes – Orry-Kelly. Based on the novel *The Maltese Falcon* by Dashiell Hammett. Working titles for this film included *The Man With The Black Hat*. Cast: Bette Davis, Warren William, Alison Skipworth, Arthur Treacher, Winifred Shaw, Marie Wilson, Porter Hall.

32 *MARKED WOMAN* – Warner Brothers 1937. 96 minutes. Executive Producers – Jack Warner and Hal Wallis. Director – Lloyd Bacon. Cast: Bette Davis, Humphrey Bogart, Jane Bryan, Lola Lane, Allen Jenkins, Henry O'Neill, Eduardo Ciannelli, Isabel Jewell, Rosalind Marquis, Mayo Methot, Ben Weldon and John Litel.

33 *KID GALAHAD* – Warner Brothers 1937. 100 minutes. Producer – Hal Wallis. Director – Michael Curtiz. Music – Max Steiner. Costumes – Orry-Kelly. Cast: Edward G. Robinson, Bette Davis, Humphrey Bogart, Wayne Morris, Jane Bryan, Ben Weldon, Harry Carey, Soledad Jiminez and Harlan Tucker.

34 *THAT CERTAIN WOMAN* – Warner Brothers 1937. 91 minutes. Producer – Hal Wallis. Director – Edmund Goulding. Music – Max Steiner. Costumes – Orry-Kelly. Photography – Ernest Haller. Cast: Bette Davis, Henry Fonda, Ian Hunter, Anita Louise, Donald Crisp, Hugh O'Connell, Katherine Alexander and Ben Weldon.

35 *IT'S LOVE I'M AFTER* – Warner Brothers 1937. 90 minutes. Producer – Hal Wallis. Director – Archie Mayo. Costumes – Orry-Kelly. Cast: Leslie Howard, Bette Davis, Olivia de Havilland, Eric Blore, Patric Knowles, Spring Byington, E. E. Clive, George Barbier, Georgia Caine and Bonita Granville.

36*JEZEBEL* – Warner Brothers 1938. 104 minutes. Producer – Hal Wallis. Director – William Wyler. Music – Max Steiner, Costumes – Orry-Kelly. Photography – Ernest Haller. This film won Bette her second Academy Award for Best Actress. Cast: Bette Davis, Henry Fonda, George Brent, Margaret Lindsay, Fay Bainter, Richard Cromwell, Donald Crisp, Henry O'Neill, John Litel, Spring Byington, Georgia Caine and Eddie Anderson.

37 *THE SISTERS* – Warner Brothers 1938. 95 minutes. Producer – Hal Wallis. Director – Anatole Litvak. Music – Max Steiner. Costumes – Orry-Kelly. Cast: Errol Flynn, Bette Davis, Anita Louise, Jane Bryan, Ian Hunter, Henry Travers, Beulah Bondi, Donald Crisp, Dick Foran, Patric Knowles, Alan Hale and Laura Hope Crewes.

38*DARK VICTORY* – Warner Brothers 1939. 105 minutes. Producer – Hal Wallis. Director – Edmund Goulding. Music – Max Steiner. Costumes – Orry-Kelly. Photography – Ernest Haller. Cast: Bette Davis, George Brent, Humphrey Bogart, Geraldine Fitzgerald, Ronald Reagan, Henry Travers and Cora Witherspoon.

39 *JUAREZ* – Warner Brothers 1939. 125 minutes. Producer – Hal Wallis. Director – William Dieterle. Screenplay – John Huston. Costumes – Orry-Kelly. Cast: Paul Muni, Bette Davis, Brian Aherne, Claude Rains, John Garfield, Donald Crisp, Gale Sondergaard, Joseph Calleia, Gilbert Roland and Henry O'Neill.

40 *THE OLD MAID* – Warner Brothers 1939. 95 minutes. Producer – Hal Wallis. Director – Edmund Goulding. Based partially on a novel by Edith Wharton, the screenplay was written by Casey Robinson after the Pulitzer Prize winning play by Zoe Atkins. Music – Max Steiner. Costumes – Orry-Kelly. Cast: Bette Davis, Miriam Hopkins, George Brent, Jane Bryan, Donald Crisp, Louise Fazenda, James Stephenson and William Lundigan.

41*THE PRIVATE LIVES OF ELIZABETH AND ESSEX* – Warner Brothers 1939. 105 minutes. Producer – Hal Wallis. Director – Michael Curtiz. Based on the play *Elizabeth The Queen* by Maxwell Anderson. Costumes – Orry-Kelly. Make-up – Perc Westmore. Cast: Bette Davis, Errol Flynn, Olivia de Havilland, Donald Crisp, Alan Hale, Vincent Price, Henry Stephenson, Nanette Fabray (listed in the credits as Nanette Fabares) and Leo G. Carroll.

42 *ALL THIS AND HEAVEN TOO* – Warner Brothers 1940. 140 minutes. Producer – Hal Wallis. Director – Anatole Litvak. Music – Max Steiner. Costumes – Orry-Kelly. Photography – Ernest Haller. Cast: Bette Davis, Charles Boyer, Jeffrey Lynn, Barbara O'Neill, Virginia Weidler, Helen Westley, Walter Hampden and June Lockhart.

43*THE LETTER* – Warner Brothers 1940. 95 minutes. Producer – Hal Wallis. Director – William Wyler. Basic on a play by Somerset Maugham, the screen treatment was written by Howard Koch. Music – Max Steiner. Costumes – Orry-Kelly. Bette was nominated for an Academy Award as Best Actress for her work in this film. Cast: Bette Davis, Herbert Marshall, James Stephenson, Freida Inescourt and Gale Sondergaard.

(bottom) With her fourth husband, Gary
Merrill in All About Eve.
(top) In The Man Who Came To Dinner
with Anne Sheridan.

44 *THE GREAT LIE* – Warner Brothers 1941. 102 minutes. Producer – Hal Wallis. Director – Edmund Goulding. Music – Max Steiner. Costumes – Orry-Kelly. The working title was *Far Horizon*. Cast: Bette Davis, George Brent, Mary Astor, Lucille Watson, Hattie McDaniel, Jerome Cowan, Charles Trowbridge and Thurston Hall.

45 *THE BRIDE CAME C.O.D.* – Warner Brothers 1941. 90 minutes. Producer – Hal Wallis. Director – William Keighley. Music – Max Steiner. Costumes – Orry-Kelly. Photography – Ernest Haller. Cast: James Cagney, Bette Davis, Stuart Erwin, Jack Carson, George Tobias, Eugene Pallette, Harry Davenport, William Frawley, Ed Brophy and William Hopper.

46* *THE LITTLE FOXES* – RKO 1941. 115 minutes. Producer – Samuel Goldwyn. Director – William Wyler. Based on the play by Lillian Hellman, the screenplay was also written by Hellman. Among the writers who worked on additional dialogue was Dorothy Parker. Musical direction – Meredith Wilson. Costumes – Orry-Kelly. Bette was nominated for the fourth time for the Academy Award of Best Actress for her work in this film. Cast: Bette Davis, Herbert Marshall, Teresa Wright, Richard Carlson, Patricia Collinge, Dan Duryea, Carl Benton Reid and Charles Dingle.

47 *THE MAN WHO CAME TO DINNER* – Warner Brothers 1941. 112 minutes. Producer – Hal Wallis. Director – William Keighley. Based on the play by George Kaufman and Moss Hart. Costumes – Orry-Kelly. Cast: Bette Davis, Ann Sheridan, Monty Woolley, Dick Travis, Jimmy Durante, Reginald Gardiner, Billy Burke, Elizabeth Fraser, Grant Mitchell and George Barbier.

48 *IN THIS OUR LIFE* – Warner Brothers 1942. 97 minutes. Producer – Hal Wallis. Director – John Huston. There is some reason to believe that Raoul Walsh also worked on this film although he is not credited. Screenplay by Howard Koch based on a Pulitzer Prize winning novel by Ellen Glasgow. Music – Max Steiner. Costumes – Orry-Kelly. Photography – Ernest Haller. Cast: Bette Davis, Olivia de Havilland, George Brent, Dennis Morgan, Charles Coburn, Frank Craven, Billie Burke and Hattie McDaniel.

49* *NOW, VOYAGER* – Warner Brothers 1942. 118 minutes. Producer – Hal Wallis. Director – Irving Rapper. Casey Robinson wrote the screenplay based on a novel by Olive Higgins Prouty. Music – Max Steiner. Costumes – Orry-Kelly. This film earned Bette her fifth nomination for a Best Actress Academy Award. Cast: Bette Davis, Paul Henreid, Claude Rains, Gladys Cooper, Bonita Granville, Ilka Chase, John Loder, Lee Patrick, James Rennie, Charles Drake and Katherine Alexander.

50* *WATCH ON THE RHINE* – Warner Brothers 1943. 114 minutes. Producer – Hal Wallis. Director – William Shumlin. Dashiell Hammett wrote the screenplay based on a play by Lillian Hellman. Additional dialogue was added by Hellman. Music – Max Steiner. Costumes – Orry-Kelly. Paul Lukas won an Academy Award for his work in this film. Cast: Bette Davis, Paul Lukas, Geraldine Fitzgerald, Lucille Watson, Beulah Bondi, George Coulouris, Donald Woods and Henry Daniel.

51 *THANK YOUR LUCKY STARS* – Warner Brothers 1943. 127 minutes. Producer – Mark Hellinger. Director – David Butler. Some songs signed Frank Loesser. Make-up – Perc Westmore. A musical review featuring a large number of cameo roles, Bette sang and danced the number "They're Either Too Young Or Too Old". Cast: Dennis Morgan, Joan Leslie, Edward Everett Horton, Humphrey Bogart, Eddie Cantor, Bette Davis, Olivia de Havilland, Errol Flynn, John Garfield, Ida Lupino, Ann Sheridan, Dinah Shore, Alexis Smith, Jack Carson, Alan Hale, George Tobias, Hattie McDaniel, Willie Best, Monte Blue and Spike Jones and His City Slickers.

52 *OLD ACQUAINTANCE* – Warner Brothers 1943. 110 minutes. Producer – Henry Blanke. Director – Vincent Sherman. Costumes – Orry-Kelly. Cast: Bette Davis, Miriam Hopkins, Gig Young, John Loder, Dolores Moran, Phillip Reed, Roscoe Karns, Anne Revere and Esther Dale.

53* *MR. SKEFFINGTON* – Warner Brothers 1944. 145 minutes. Executive Producer – Jack Warner. Produced by Philip and Julius Epstein. Director – Vincent Sherman. The screenplay was based on a novel signed simply, "Elizabeth". Costumes – Orry-Kelly, Make-up – Perc Westmore. Photography – Ernest Haller. Bette was again nominated for an Academy Award as Best Actress following this film. Cast: Bette Davis, Claude Rains, Walter Abel, Richard Waring, George Coulouris, Marjorie Riordan, Robert Shayne, John Alexander, Jerome Cowan and Johnny Mitchell.

54 *HOLLYWOOD CANTEEN* – Warner Brothers 1944. 123 minutes. Producer – Alex Gottlieb. Director: Delmer Daves. A war-effort film, the cast included a large number of cameo roles from the Andrews Sisters, Jack Benny, Joe E. Brown, Eddie Cantor, Joan Crawford, Bette Davis, John Garfield, Sydney Greenstreet, Paul Henreid, Peter Lorre, Ida Lupino, Irene Manning, Janis Paige, Eleanor Parker, Roy Rogers and Trigger, S. Z. Sakall, Zachary Scott, Alexis Smith, Barbara Stanwyck, Craig Stevens, Jane Wyman, Donald Woods, Jimmy Dorsey and his Orchestra, Carmen Cavallaeo and his Orchestra, The Golden Gate Quartet, and The Sons Of The Pioneers.

55* *THE CORN IS GREEN* – Warner Brothers 1945. 115 minutes. Producer – Jack Chertok. Director – Irving Rapper. Screenplay by Casey Robinson based on a play by Emlyn Williams. Music – Max Steiner. Costumes – Orry-Kelly. Cast: Bette Davis, John Dall, Joan Lorring, Nigel Bruce, Rhys Williams, Rosalind Ivan and Mildred Dunnock.

56 *A STOLEN LIFE* – Warner Brothers 1946. 109 minutes. Producer – Bette Davis. Director – Curtis Bernhardt. Music – Max Steiner. Costumes – Orry-Kelly. Photography – Ernest Haller. Produced by Bette herself, under the name of B.D. Productions, she was not only able to hire the people she most admired working with but also cast herself in the role of twins. The split-screen technique used so that the twins could do scenes together was the most advanced at the time. Cast: Bette Davis, Glenn Ford, Dane Clark, Walter Brennan, Charles Ruggles, Bruce Bennett, Peggy Knudsen, Esther Dale, James Flavin and Monte Blue.

57 *DECEPTION* – Warner Brothers 1946. 110 minutes. Producer – Henry Blanke. Director – Irving Rapper. Based on a play by Louis Verneuil. Hollenius' Cello Concerto by Erich Wolfgang Korngold. Photography – Ernest Haller. Cast: Bette Davis, Paul Henreid, Claude Rains, John Abbott, Benson Fong, Richard Walsh and Suzi Crandall.

58 *WINTER MEETING* – Warner Brothers 1948. 104 minutes. Producer – Henry Blanke. Director – Bretaigne Windust. Music – Max Steiner. Photography – Ernest Haller. Make-up – Perc Westmore. Cast: Bette Davis, Janis Paige, Jim Davis, John Hoyt, Florence Bates, Walter Baldwin and Ransom Sherman.

59 *JUNE BRIDE* – Warner Brothers 1948. 96 minutes. Producer – Henry Blanke. Director – Bretaigne Windust. Costumes – Edith Head. Make-up – Perc Westmore. Cast: Bette Davis, Robert Montgomery, Fay Bainter, Betty Lynn, Tom Tully, Barbara Bates, Jerome Cowan and Debbie Reynolds.

60 *BEYOND THE FOREST* – Warner Brothers 1949. 97 minutes. Producer – Henry Blanke. Director – King Vidor. Music – Max Steiner. Costumes – Edith Head. Make-up – Perc Westmore. The film was condemned by the Catholic Church and an edited version which ran two minutes shorter than the original was circulated to gain Church acceptance. Cast: Bette Davis, Joseph Cotton, David Brian, Ruth Roman, Minor Watson, Dona Drake and Regis Toomey.

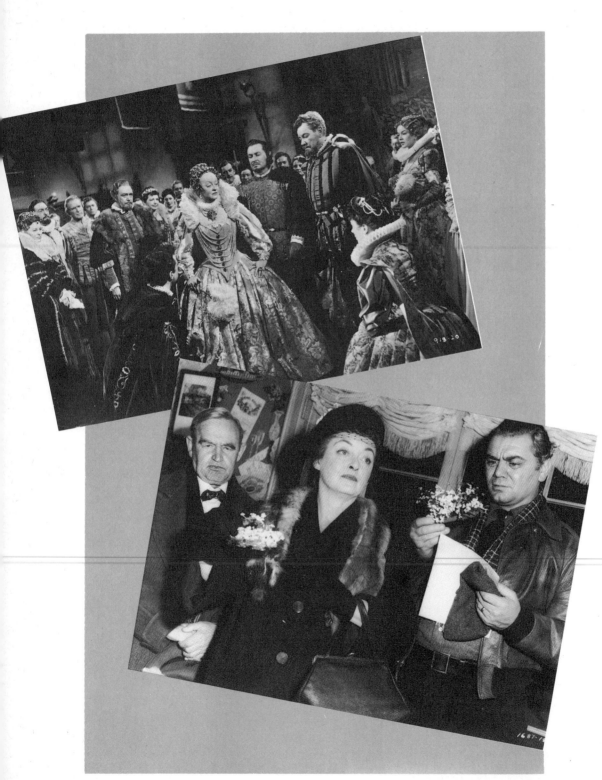

(top) The Virgin Queen *with Richard Todd, Joan Collins and Herbert Marshall.*

(bottom) In her favourite role as Aggie Hurley in The Catered Affair *with Ernest Borgnine (right) and Barry Fitzgerald.*

61* *ALL ABOUT EVE* – Twentieth Century Fox 1950. 138 minutes. Producer – Darryl Zanuck. Director – Joseph L. Mankiewicz. Some costumes designed by Edith Head. Bette was nominated yet again as Best Actress for an Academy Award. Cast: Bette Davis, Anne Baxter, George Sanders, Celeste Holm, Gary Merrill (whom Bette married shortly after the picture was completed), Hugh Marlowe, Thelma Ritter, Marilyn Monroe, Gregory Ratoff, Barbara Bates, Randy Stuart and Eddie Fisher (who played a small role in the film but was edited out of the final version).

62 *PAYMENT ON DEMAND* – RKO 1951. 91 minutes. Producers – Jack Skirball and Bruce Manning. Director – Curtis Bernhardt. Bette's costumes were designed by Edith Head. Because Howard Hughes didn't like the original ending of the film, it had to be changed. He insisted it be a happier ending. Jane Cowl died before shooting was finished. Cast: Bette Davis, Barry Sullivan, Jane Cowl, Kent Taylor, Betty Lynn, John Sutton, Frances Dee, Peggy Castle and Otto Kruger.

63 *ANOTHER MAN'S POISON* – United Artists 1952. 88 minutes. Producers, Douglas Fairbank, Jr. and Daniel Angel. Director, Irving Rapper. Screenplay by Val Guest after the play *Deadlock* by Leslie Sands. This was Bette's first English-produced film. Cast: Bette Davis, Gary Merrill, Emlyn Williams, Anthony Steele, Barbara Murray, Reginald Beckwith and Edna Morris.

64 *PHONE CALL FROM A STRANGER* – Twentieth Century Fox 1952. 96 minutes. Producer – Nunnally Johnson. Director – Jean Negulesco. Bette made a cameo appearance and received special billing. Cast: Shelley Winters, Gary Merrill, Michael Rennie, Keenan Wynn, Evelyn Varden, Craig Stevens, Warren Stevens and Bette Davis.

65* *THE STAR* – Friedlob Productions released by Twentieth Century Fox 1952. 90 minutes. Producer – Bert Friedlob. Director – Stuart Heisler. Bette's costumes by Orry-Kelly. Her portrayal in this film of Margaret Elliott earned her another Academy Award nomination as Best Actress. Cast: Bette Davis, Sterling Hayden, Natalie Wood, Warner Anderson, Minor Watson, June Travis, Katherine Warren and Paul Frees.

66* *THE VIRGIN QUEEN* – Twentieth Century Fox 1955. 92 minutes. Producer – Charles Brackett. Director – Henry Koster. Make-up – Perc Westmore. This is Bette again playing Queen Elizabeth I, with her hairline shaved back the way it was sixteen years before when she first played the role. Cast: Bette Davis, Richard Todd, Joan Collins, Herbert Marshall, Dan O'Herlihy, Robert Douglas, Romney Brent and Rod Taylor.

67 *STORM CENTER* – Phoenix Productions released by Columbia Pictures, 1956. 86 minutes. Producer – Julian Blaustein. Director – Daniel Taradish. Working titles included *This Time Tomorrow* and *The Library*. Cast: Bette Davis, Brian Keith, Kim Hunter, Paul Kelly, Kevin Caughlin, Joe Mantell and Sallie Brophie.

68* *THE CATERED AFFAIR* – MGM 1956. 92 minutes. Producer – Sam Zimbalist. Director – Richard Brooks. Screenplay by Gore Vidal after a play written for television by Paddy Chayefsky. Music – Andre Previn. The Aggie Conlon Hurley role that Bette portrayed is one she has often said to be her favourite. Cast: Bette Davis, Ernest Borgnine, Debbie Reynolds, Barry Fitzgerald, Rod Taylor, Robert Simon, Madge Kennedy, Dorothy Stickney and Mae Clarke.

69 *JOHN PAUL JONES* – Samuel Bronston Productions distributed by Warner Brothers 1959. 126 minutes. Producer – Samuel Bronston. Director – John Farrow. Screenplay by John Farrow and Jesse Lasky, Jr. Music – Max Steiner. Shot mainly in Spain, Bette's scenes were filmed at Versailles in France. Cast: Robert Stack, Marisa Pavan, Charles Coburn, Erin O'Brien, Bette Davis, Macdonald Carey, Jean-Pierre Aumont, David Farrar, Peter Cushing, Bruce Cabot, Tom Brennum, Susana Canales and Jorge Riviere.

70 *THE SCAPEGOAT* – Du Maurier-Guinness Productions distributed by MGM 1959. 92 minutes. Producer – Michael Balcon. Director – Robert Hamer. Based on a novel by Daphne Du Maurier. The screenplay was adapted by Gore Vidal. Filmed in England. Cast: Alec Guinness, Bette Davis, Nicole Maurey, Irene Worth, Pamela Brown, Annabel Bartlett, Geoffrey Keen, Noel Howlett, Peter Bull, Leslie French and Alan Web.

71 *POCKETFUL OF MIRACLES* – Franton Productions released by United Artists 1961. 136 minutes. Producer – Frank Capra. Associate Producers – Glenn Ford and Joseph Sistrom. Director – Frank Capra. Based on a story by Damon Runyon. Some costumes by Edith Head. Title song by James Van Heusen and Sammy Cahn. Cast: Glenn Ford, Bette Davis, Hope Lange, Arthur O'Connell, Peter Falk, Thomas Mitchell, Edward Everett Horton, Mickey Shaughnessy, David Brian and Sheldon Leonard.

72* *WHAT EVER HAPPENED TO BABY JANE?* – Seven Arts Associates/Robert Aldrich Production released by Warner Brothers 1962. 132 minutes. Executive Producer – Kenneth Hyman. Director and Associate Producer – Robert Aldrich. Photography – Ernest Haller. Bette received her ninth Academy Award nomination for her role in this film. Her daughter B. D. Merrill played a small role. Cast: Bette Davis, Joan Crawford, Victor Buono, Marjorie Bennett, Maidie Norman, Anna Lee, Julie Allred, Gina Gillespie, Dave Willcock, Ann Barton and Barbara Merrill.

73 *DEAD RINGER* – Warner Brothers 1964. 115 minutes. Producer – William H. Wright. Director – Paul Henreid. Music – Andre Previn. Photography – Ernest Haller. This was the last picture Haller shot with Bette as he died shortly after the film was completed. The British title was *Dead Image*. Cast: Bette Davis, Karl Malden, Peter Lawford, Philip Carey, Jean Hagen, George Macready, Estelle Winwood and Monica Henreid (Paul's daughter).

74 *THE EMPTY CANVAS* – Joseph E. Levine/Carlo Ponti Production released by Embassy Pictures 1964. 118 minutes. Producer – Carlo Ponti. Director – Damiano Damiani. Based on a novel by Alberto Moravia. Cast: Bette Davis, Horst Buchholz, Catherine Spaak, Isa Mirandi, Lea Padovani, Daniela Rocca and Georges Wilson.

75 *WHERE LOVE HAS GONE* – Joseph E. Levine Production released by Paramount 1964. 114 minutes. Producer – Joseph E. Levine. Director – Edward Dymtryk. Based on a novel by Harold Robbins. Costumes – Edith Head. Title song by James Van Heusen and Sammy Cahn. Paramount's insistence that Bette film a new ending for this film resulted in a law suit against her which the studio eventually lost. Cast: Susan Hayward, Bette Davis, Michael Connors, Joey Heatherton, Jane Greer, DeForrest Kelly, George Macready and Anne Seymour.

76 *HUSH . . . HUSH, SWEET CHARLOTTE* – Associates/Aldrich Production released by Twentieth Century Fox 1964. 134 minutes. Producer and director – Robert Aldrich. Joan Crawford was originally cast for the role of Miriam but fell ill during the shooting and was replaced by Olivia de Havilland. Cast: Bette Davis, Olivia de Havilland, Joseph Cotton, Agnes Moorehead, Cecil Kellaway, Victor Buono, Mary Astor, Bruce Dern and George Kennedy.

77 *THE NANNY* – Seven Arts/Hammer Films released by Twentieth Century Fox 1965. 93 minutes. Producer – Jimmy Sangster. Director – Seth Holt. Filmed in England. Cast: Bette Davis, Wendy Craig, Jill Bennett, James Villiers, William Dix, Pamela Franklin, Jack Watling, Maurice Denham, Alfred Burke, Nora Gordon, Sandra Power, Harry Fowler and Angharad Aubrey.

78 *THE ANNIVERSARY* – Seven Arts/Hammer Films released by Twentieth Century Fox 1968. 95 minutes. Producer – Jimmy Sangster. Director – Roy Ward Baker. The original director was Alvin Rakoff but he was replaced during the shooting. Filmed in England. Cast: Bette Davis, Sheila Hancock, Jack Hedley, James Cossins, Christine Roberts, Elaine Taylor, Timothy Bateson and Arnold Diamond.

79 *CONNECTING ROOMS* – London Screen Distributors released by Hemdale 1971. 103 minutes. Producer – Harry Field. Director – Franklin Gollings. Filmed in England. Cast: Bette Davis, Michael Redgrave, Alexis Kanner, Kay Walsh, Gabrielle Drake, Olga Georges-Picot, Leo Genn, Richard Wyler, Brian Wilde, John Woodnutt, Tony Hughes, Mark Jones and James Maxwell.

80 *BUNNY O'HARE* – American International Pictures 1971. 92 minutes. Producers James Nicholson and Samuel Arkoff. Director – Gerd Oswald. Cast: Bette Davis, Ernest Borgnine, Jack Cassidy, Joan Delaney, Jay Robinson, John Astin and Reva Rose.

81 *LO SCOPONE SCIENTIFICO (The Scientific Cardplayer* or *The Game)* – C.I.C. Productions 1972. 113 minutes. Producer – Dino De Laurentis. Director – Luigi Comencini. Made in Italy basically for an Italian audience. Cast: Alberto Sordi, Silvana Mangano, Joseph Cotton, Bette Davis, Domenico Modugno and Mario Carotenuto.

82 *BURNT OFFERINGS* – United Artists 1976. 116 minutes. Producer and director – Dan Curtis. Cast: Karen Black, Oliver Reed, Burgess Meredith, Eileen Heckart, Lee Montgomery, Dub Taylor and Bette Davis.

83 *DEATH ON THE NILE* – Columbia-EMI-Warner 1978. 140 minutes. Producers – John Brabourne and Richard Goodwin. Director – John Guillermin. Based on a novel by Agatha Christie. Filmed on location in Egypt and England. Cast: Peter Ustinov, David Niven, Bette Davis, Mia Farrow, George Kennedy, Jack Warden, Jane Birkin, Maggie Smith and Angela Lansbury.

84 *RETURN FROM WITCH MOUNTAIN* – Buena Vista (Walt Disney Productions) 1978. 93 minutes. Producers – Ron Miller and Jerry Courtland. Director – John Hough. Cast: Bette Davis, Christopher Lee, Kim Richards, Ike Eisemann, Jack Soo, Dick Bakalyan, Ward Costello and Anthony James.

85 *WATCHER IN THE WOODS* – Buena Vista (Walt Disney Productions) 1980. 107 minutes. Producers – Ron Miller and Tom Leetch. Director – John Hough. Cast: Bette Davis, Carroll Baker, David McCallum, Lynn-Holly Johnson, Ian Bannen and Kyle Richards.

THEATRICAL EXPERIENCE

Spring 1928. THE FAMOUS MRS. FARE – Directed by James Light of the Provincetown Playhouse, Greenwich Village, New York for the John Murray Anderson School.

Spring 1928. BROADWAY – Directed by George Cukor, Cukor/Kondolf Company, Rochester, New York.

Summer 1928. THE CHARM SCHOOL – The Junior Players, East Dennis, Mass.

Summer 1928. MR. PIM PASSES BY – The Cape Playhouse, Dennis, Mass.

Summer 1928. THE SILVER CHORD – The Cape Playhouse, Dennis, Mass.

Autumn 1928. Repertory – Cukor/Kondolf Company, Rochester, New York. Plays included, *EXCESS BAGGAGE, CRADLE SNATCHERS, LAFF THAT OFF, THE MAN WHO CAME BACK* and *YELLOW.*

Winter 1928-1929. THE EARTH BETWEEN – Provincetown Playhouse, Greenwich Village, New York.

Spring 1929. THE WILD DUCK and *LADY FROM THE SEA* on tour with Blanche Yurka.

Summer 1929. Cape Playhouse, Dennis, Mass. Plays included *THE CONSTANT WIFE, THE PATSY* and *YOU CAN NEVER TELL.*

Winter 1929. BROKEN DISHES – on Broadway.

Summer 1930. Cape Playhouse, Dennis, Mass. No list of plays available.

Autumn 1930. BROKEN DISHES – on tour.

Autumn 1930. SOLID SOUTH – on Broadway.

1952. TWO'S COMPANY – including Broadway.

1959-1960. On tour with *THE WORLD OF CARL SANDBURG* including Broadway.

1961-1962. THE NIGHT OF THE IGUANA – on Broadway.

1974. MISS MOFFAT – on Broadway.

1975. AN INFORMAL EVENING WITH BETTE DAVIS – Sydney, Australia and London, England.

MOVIES MADE EXPRESSLY FOR TELEVISION

MADAME SIN – Produced by Robert Wagner. Directed by David Greene. Wagner financed this with Sir Lew Grade, the original idea being that the film would serve as a pilot for a television series. It was eventually released in Europe as a feature film although in the United States it's been shown only on television. First aired January 15, 1972.

THE JUDGE AND JAKE WYLER – Directed by David Lowell Rich. First filmed as a series pilot, additional footage was added on to fill the time requirement of a film for television. First aired December 2, 1972.

SCREAM PRETTY PEGGY – Directed by Gordon Hessler. First aired November 24, 1973.

THE DISAPPEARANCE OF AIME – Directed by Anthony Harvey. First aired November 17, 1976.

THE DARK SECRET OF HARVEST HOME – Directed by Leon Penn. Aired in two parts – January 23 and January 24, 1978.

STRANGERS – THE STORY OF A MOTHER AND DAUGHTER – Directed by Milton Katselas. First aired May 13, 1979.

WHITE MAMMA – First aired March 5, 1980, CBS.

SKYWARD – Directed by Ron Howard. First aired November 20, 1980, CBS.

FAMILY REUNION – Directed By Fielder Cook. First aired 11 & 12 October, 1981.